The M & E Higher Business Educ

CW00361280

International Marketing

General Editor

Dr Edwin Kerr
*Chief Officer, Council for National
Academic Awards*

Advisory Editors

K.W. Aitken
*Vice-Principal, South-East
London College*

P.W. Holmes
*Director, Regional Management
Studies Centre, Bristol Polytechnic*

The M & E Higher Business Education Series

International Marketing

Professor J. Aidan O'Reilly

BComm, MBA, MHCIMA

Dean of the Faculty of Business and Management,
University of Ulster

Macdonald and Evans

Macdonald & Evans Ltd
Estover, Plymouth PL6 7PZ

First published 1985

©Macdonald & Evans Ltd 1985

British Library Cataloguing in Publication Data

O'Reilly, J. Aiden
    International marketing.—(The M & E higher
    business education series, ISSN 0265–8801)
    1. Export marketing—Great Britain
    I. Title
    658.8'48'0941   HF1009.5

ISBN 0–7121–0972–2

Filmset by J&L Composition Ltd,
Filey, N. Yorkshire
Printed in Great Britain by
Hollen Street Press Ltd., Slough

Foreword

In recent years business practice has been undergoing major and fundamental changes for a variety of economic, social and technological reasons.
In parallel with these changes the developments in education for business
at all levels have also been extensive and far-reaching. In particular this is
true at the advanced levels for courses leading to (*a*) the first degrees of the
Council for National Academic Awards and of the universities, (*b*) the
higher awards of the Business and Technician Education Council and its
Scottish equivalent, and (*c*) examinations of the relevant professional
bodies. Many such courses are now offered in educational institutions
which include the polytechnics, the universities, the colleges and institutes
of higher education, the further education colleges and the Scottish central
institutions. In addition to these developments in curricular design there
have been important advances in educational and teaching methods.

Macdonald & Evans already have a large involvement in meeting the
needs of students and staff in business education through their Business
Studies series and HANDBOOK series. The publishers have now decided
to complement these with their Higher Business Education series.

The new series is intended to be one of major educational significance
and will cover all aspects of higher business education. It will be designed
for student and staff use with all of the advanced courses at all of the
educational institutions mentioned above. Each book in the series will
have both a planned part in the series and be complete in itself, and each
will adopt a thematic and problem-solving approach.

The editorial team have chosen authors who are experienced people
from technological institutions and from professional practice and will
collaborate with them to ensure that the books are authoritative and
written in a style which will make them easy to use and which will assist the
students to learn effectively from such use.

The editorial team will welcome criticisms on each of the books so that
improvements may be made at the reprint stages to ensure a closer
achievement of the objectives of the books and all the series.

Edwin Kerr
General Editor

Preface

This text aims to provide a framework for international marketing and its context in the modern business world. It is designed to give the reader an understanding of the various facets of international marketing in a systematic and logical form, and to stimulate him to explore further the various challenges to this key area of activity. Through judicious use of the text and questions, he will have the opportunity to develop and evaluate a range of alternative approaches to vital issues in international marketing.

Learning is concerned with the development of:

(a) a positive attitude;
(b) precise areas of knowledge; and
(c) appropriate skills.

This book seeks to make a real contribution to the knowledge component. As with many texts, there is a more limited contribution to the attitude and skills elements. However, the reader may acquire some important insights into the kind of positive thinking attitude and export planning skills required by participation in group discussion and analysis, following individual study of the export exercises and case studies outlined in the text.

It is assumed that the student already has an understanding of basic marketing principles, although the opening chapter gives an outline of these and their applications. This is followed by a chapter on the key role and initiatives of international marketing in the contemporary world of business. The process of planning and developing international marketing activities is then discussed chronologically, from the point of view of a medium-sized company. However, the reader is assisted by brief but relevant examples from a range of industries and in a variety of settings.

The learning experience made available from this book, therefore, consists of three elements:

(a) the text itself;
(b) the examples relating practice to theory; and
(c) the questions at the end of each chapter which challenge the effectiveness of this integration.

It is hoped to stimulate the interest of readers in further potential developments in international marketing. Some of these issues are raised in the final chapter.

It should be noted that export marketing and international marketing are used synonymously in the book and that the use of he/him is purely for convenience of presentation.

1985   J.A.O'R.

Acknowledgments

The very helpful advice and assistance of many people was necessary in the completion of this book.

I am particularly grateful to: Mr Jim Dowds, Chairman and Chief Executive of CU Products (NI) Ltd.; Mr Cyril Kerr, Chief Executive, Datac Controls Ltd.; and Mr Nicky Hertery, Chief Executive, Verbatim Ltd., for assistance with their case studies. My thanks also to the Irish Management Institute for their assistance with the case study section.

My thanks also to the British Overseas Trade Board, the Irish Export Board and the Thailand Ministry of Commerce, for the reproduction of material in the book.

My thanks must also be given to Mr Jim Bell and Mr Brendan Kelleher of the Ulster Polytechnic, for their specialist advice and assistance. The work of the part-time Master of Business Administration Year II students at the Ulster Polytechnic is also gratefully acknowledged, especially Brian Anderson, David Bingham, Jim Bradshaw, Alan Doig, F. Coulter, Des Holmes, John Keanie, Hans Martin, Margaret McKenna and Paul Sinte.

Finally, my thanks to Miss Gillian Webb and Mrs Carol Murtagh for all their help and support.

Contents

Marketing Concepts and Their Applications

OBJECTIVES

Ideally, before studying international marketing, the reader should have some understanding of the basics of marketing. However, it is often the case that this is not possible and that for many people marketing is confused with sales and selling. For these reasons, it is considered prudent that this first chapter should have as its objectives the provision of:

    (*a*) an understanding of marketing concepts;
    (*b*) an outline of relevant aspects of contemporary society; and
    (*c*) an opportunity to study the relationship between those concepts and society.

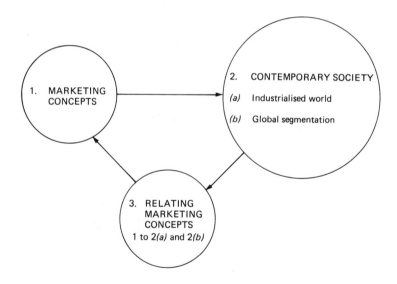

Fig. 1. *Framework for study.*

Figure 1 gives this sequence of organisation.

MARKETING CONCEPTS

Marketing defined

Many readers who have read other books on marketing will have studied the debate on the *marketing concept*, and the various definitions of marketing. These definitions include the following.

"Marketing is the management process responsible for identifying, anticipating and satisfying customer requirements, profitably." (Institute of Marketing.)

"Marketing is the set of human activities directed at facilitating and consummating exchanges." (Kotler: *Marketing Management*.)

"Marketing—the performance of business activities that direct the flow of goods or services from producer to consumer or user." (Converse, Hugey and Mitchell: *Elements of Marketing*.)

For the purposes of this chapter and this book, and for readers still unsure of their basic marketing, some brief discussion is useful here.

Marketing might be comprehensively defined as those *processes* which contribute to the *identification*, *selection*, *communication* and *satisfaction* of the product or service needs of consumers or companies, through the management of limited resources: men, money, materials, machinery, media and systems (internal to the company, and external—industrial, political, legal and social). The following summary might assist with the understanding of those processes.

(*a*) **Consumer needs.**   *Products:* Durable—houses
                                                 motor cars
                              Consumable—food
                                         clothes

                             Services: Entertainment
                                         Leisure

(*b*) **Company needs.**   *Products:* Components
     (industrial
     products and   Trucks/vans/office equipment
     services)

                             Services: Maintenance/cleaning, etc.

Marketing
- Identification ⎫
- Selection ⎭ Market research
- Communication: Potential supplier / Potential customer / Promotion
- Satisfaction: Production / Pricing / Placing/distribution / Selling/delivery

It is important to understand the *comprehensiveness* of these processes. The reader should note that the selling process is just a *small* (but *vital*) part of the total marketing picture.

The marketing concept

Marketing has often been described as "A genuine attention to customers' needs and wants".

The distinction should be made at this point between needs and wants. The needs of a company or a person, it might be argued, are something *deeper* than wants, and often emerge only after an investigation/discussion between the potential customer and potential supplier. A company might *want* a computer, but its needs will probably include a precisely defined management information system, incorporating a particular computer system which will only be identified after some investigation. Many small firms fall into the trap of "buying a micro" without a proper objective investigation of their needs before making the purchase, which should incorporate a system, software, training and after-sales service.

It is often argued that when sales are difficult and costly to make, i.e. the process of converting needs to *wants* is "uphill", then perhaps the definition of the needs has been faulty, and more effort should have been put into the accuracy of identification/selection—the first stage of the marketing process. In other words, the more effective the marketing, the less difficult and costly the sales/selling (*see* Fig. 2).

It follows from the above discussion of the marketing concept that the more satisfaction given to the customer, the more the sales and profitability of the supplier.

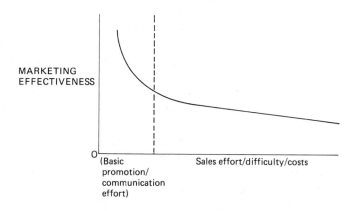

Fig. 2. *Marketing effectiveness and sales effort.*

Integrated marketing

There is a theory that marketing can pervade the whole range of business activities such as R & D, production, finance and personnel, particularly the attitude of satisfying customer and industrial needs. As Drucker states in *The Practice of Management*, "Marketing is not only much broader than selling, it is not a specialised activity at all. It encompasses the entire business. It is the whole business seen from the point of view of its final result, that is from the customer's point of view. Concern and responsibility for marketing must therefore permeate all areas of the enterprise."

There are many associated concepts—buyer behaviour and taste, product presentation and packaging, and the promotion/communication selection process, including persuasion concepts.

The environment

It follows from the marketing concept that the environment plays a most central role in the planning and operation of the producing company. It is important, therefore, to attempt to understand that environment at a micro as well as a macro level. There is much secondary data available about population trends and structure at local, regional, national and international levels. It is important to seek to understand these trends and *anticipate* changes, and the rate of change. However, an often neglected dimension of the investigation exercise is the detailed study of the micro picture, i.e. *what*, *why*, *how*, *where* and *when* does the *individual* household or company buyer make the respective purchase? What need is being met, how was that need identified, where would that buyer look/read/ search to seek to satisfy that need? Thus the whole area of individual and small group (family/company) buying behaviour and decision-making is most important.

A FRAMEWORK OF CONTEMPORARY SOCIETY

In the above section, the importance of the environment was stressed in the making of the exchange "bargain": *satisfaction* to *customer* on one side of the scale being the equivalent to *profit* to the *supplier* on the other side of the scale.

It is now proposed briefly to outline some aspects of contemporary society, first in terms of the industrialised world and then from a more holistic global perspective. Irrespective of geographical location, the producing company may be said to have to relate to various environments and societal trends. These may include political, legal, social, economic and technological environments. Figure 3 may assist with later analysis.

This framework applies equally to the least developed, developing and industrialised parts of the world. However, in the first instance, it is intended to examine some aspects of societal trends in the industrialised world. Most producing companies pay close attention to political changes in various countries, and their impact is monitored through the media and individual company/industry studies. This is also true for legal, technological and economic changes. In fact, many are documented and related to one another. However, social changes tend to be:

(*a*) quite complex;
(*b*) multi-dimensional; and
(*c*) often less well documented.

It is proposed here to comment on some selected trends by way of illustration. It is most important to note that these will not affect all production companies to the same extent. Other trends not discussed here may be much more relevant, e.g. marital breakdown, single-parent families, rising levels of youth unemployment, working wives, changes in levels and methods of education and health care, etc.

Fig. 3. *External influences on producing company.*

Many issues now face the producing company in the environment of the industrialised world. Some of the most central include consumerism, marketing ethics and social responsibility, but other forces have effects which can be established in varying degrees; e.g. environmentalism, shortages, inflation, recession and legislation. These are briefly examined below.

Consumerism
Consumerism is a demand that asks that marketers give greater attention to consumer wants and desires in making their decisions, with regard to not only product offerings, but also their quality of life and the long-term effects of the firm's actions.

Consumerism is a protest against malpractice and abuses. The growing interest in this subject, plus the activities of a few unscrupulous "businessmen", have brought increased legislation and regulatory measures intended to give the consumer more protection. Consumerism has brought to the attention of the marketers the feelings of the buyers that:

(*a*) marketing costs are too high;

(*b*) the market system is inefficient;

(*c*) marketers are guilty of collusion and price fixing;

(*d*) product quality and service are poor;

(*e*) the marketing system has produced health and safety hazards;

(*f*) consumers do not receive complete information;

(*g*) design flaws are not always remedied.

If these challenges are to be recognised as important, business attitudes will change and result in companies being more responsible towards the market. The consumer movement, now international, is a powerful lobby with specific proposals including: truth-in-lending; unit pricing; ingredient labelling; open dating; and truth-in-advertising.

Marketing ethics

Robert Bartels sees the evolution of marketing ethics as follows:

> Standards derive from the culture, from various institutional processes and structures, and from the expectations nurtured among the economic participants. With determinable standards, one must select a course of particular action.

> He is guided by the level of his ethical sensitivity, by the strength of complementary and contrasting claims, and finally in some instances by economic capacity to act.

The marketers will therefore develop their own ethics, dependent upon their perception. The marketer can be seen to have an "individual", an "organisational" or a "professional" ethic, a choice which faces the marketer every day. Howard Bowen records these questions:

> Should he conduct selling in ways that intrude on the privacy of people, for example by door-to-door selling?

> Should he use methods involving ballyhoo, chances, prizes, hawling and other tactics, which are at least of doubtful good taste?

> Should he employ "high pressure" tactics in persuading people to buy?

> Should he try to hasten the obsolescence of goods by bringing out an endless succession of new models and new styles?

> Should he appeal to and attempt to strengthen the motives of materialism, invidious consumption, and "keeping up with the Jones's?"

Ultimately, each marketer must choose and practise a philosophy of proper behaviour. Every moral system is predicated on some conception of the good life, and the relation of one's welfare to that of others. The abundance of opportunities in contemporary society, opening up as a result of technological advances and the continued development of world markets, will test the marketers in their successful exploitations under an "ethical" practice.

Social responsibility

Traditionally, customers, investors and employees were considered as being important elements as far as businessmen and marketers were concerned. However, contemporary society considers that this statement alone does not constitute socially responsible objectives. It is also important to consider:

(*a*) the relationship between social responsibility in marketing and the profit motive;

(*b*) the process for making socially responsible decisions in the organisations attempting to market their products.

Marketers and consumers now readily accept that business must be concerned with the "quality" of life, in addition to the quantification by which market performance has traditionally been measured. This requires that consideration be given to: low income groups and their requirements; profit levels reaped; the charging of more than the true value; price discriminations; price collusion; the warning of price changes, both upwards and downwards; and the disclosure of available price discounts.

It is also a matter of debate as to who should be specifically accountable for the social considerations involved in marketing decisions. Is it a district sales manager, a staff marketing department, the marketing director or the board of directors? The most likely answer in this debate is that, at the very least, all members of the marketing organisation are accountable for the societal aspects of their decisions, and should be so in regard to future generations as well as present society.

Other considerations

The ecological questions articulated by the environmentalist lobby revolve around several aspects including: planned obsolescence; pollution; recycling waste materials; and preservation of resources. These issues are raised in an attempt to minimise the harm done to the environment and quality of life by marketing practices, including, possibly, intervention in consumer wants which, if satisfied, would incur unwanted environmental cost.

Recent history has brought to our attention the very real possibility of *shortages* in basic commodities, and marketers have two basic options:

(*a*) to demarket, buying up all available supplies and exploiting their existing position to create what amounts to instant profits or;

(*b*) to adopt a marketing-as-usual approach, maintaining the regularity of the situation, holding on to customers and profits.

However, another alternative is also possible in that a real market-orientated company will strive to assist its customers in solving their problems.

It is important to note that the marketing concept has also been successfully applied to the service industries such as education, health and consultancy. Other recent applications have been in the areas of national professional organisations and institutions such as political parties, museums and other cultural and entertainment centres. Religious organisations and family planning organisations are other examples. There are many instances of these applications in the United States, Europe and the Third World, where population management has been a major challenge for many countries.

Inflation has become a major economic and social problem, and will probably remain so. High levels of inflation will require the application of the best possible skills in the marketer's portfolio to maximise the benefits for the business and the consumer. However, to ensure continuity of the business, and its services to the consumer, profit protection must be the cardinal aim, and all strategies must be given consideration in pursuit of this aim.

Within the last decade or so, most developed countries will have experienced *shortage, inflation and recession*, and consumers will have exhibited the typical spending pattern in the circumstances, namely they:

(*a*) continue to consume freely; or
(*b*) develop a concentration upon their functional requirements; or
(*c*) actually contract consumption if not actually de-consume.

Fig. 4. *The North/South divide.*

This scenario will, in effect, take the marketer back to basics—finding out what is needed and offering it.

In the context of the major current issues discussed earlier, and the forces outlined above, there has been an underlying trend of *increased regulation*, including formal legislation by government. Marketers need continually to be aware of the impact upon their ability to support the market system.

The Brandt reports on *North/South—A Programme for Survival* provide a useful framework for a global perspective in terms of the challenge and opportunities for intercourse and trade between the least developed, developing and industrialised regions of the world. These reports should be essential background reading for imaginative international marketers. The "north/south" divide is shown in Fig. 4.

The analysis of various environments is just as relevant to the under-developed regions of the world, where 80 per cent of the world's population attempt to subsist on 20 per cent of its wealth. However, it is important to note that various regions and countries are at different stages of the "development life cycle" (*see* Fig. 5), based on the concept of the *product*

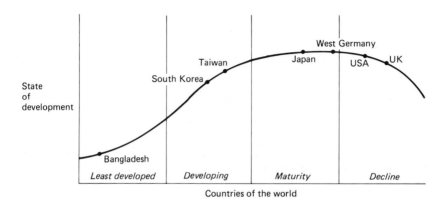

Fig. 5. *Development life cycle.*

life cycle. The major challenges vary from starvation/food/nourishment to agricultural development to industrialisation/intermediate technology. There is no doubt that, if there is good liaison with international funding agencies such as the United Nations, the World Bank and the World Health Organisation, together with bilateral agreements, market opportunities do exist, based on sound study of the local culture and its needs. This will in many cases mean special product/systems adaptation, or initial special development/consultancy projects.

SUMMARY

A wide range of social and economic changes have had an impact on the marketing concept, which has developed to the point where, within a business, it is no longer regarded as a supplementary activity to be performed after the production process has been accomplished. It is all-pervasive and this has been essential to ensure continuity of the business in the dynamic environment which is the market today. The changing of society brings about a constantly evolving craft and discipline in marketing, and differences in society's idea of what constitutes effective and socially responsible marketing.

One of the most crucial tasks facing marketing as a business discipline is undoubtedly the resolution of the major issues—consumerism, marketing ethics and social responsibility. The survival of the competitive market system could depend upon the resolution of the questions being raised in these areas, and it is likely that we shall see increased regulation, better consumer information, and a more socially responsible marketing philosophy.

Some of the interesting developments of the marketing concept include its many applications to the service industry and non-profit-making organisations.

QUESTIONS

1. Examine on paper what the application of the marketing concept should mean to:

(*a*) a local store/manufacturer;
(*b*) a local bank manager;
(*c*) a local technical college?

2. State how you would advise a manufacturer of timber-frame houses to apply the marketing concept to:

(*a*) the United Kingdom; and
(*b*) a developing country such as Thailand.

CHAPTER TWO

The Key Role of International Marketing

OBJECTIVES

The aim of this chapter is to ensure that the reader has:
  (a) a greater awareness of the key role of international marketing in the modern world;
  (b) a broad understanding of international marketing and its impact on international relations, including the role of international agencies; and
  (c) an insight into how international marketing affects people, company, industry, country and trade bloc.

DEVELOPMENT OF INTERNATIONAL MARKETING

International trade and international marketing have their origins in many ancient civilisations. When barter, involving an exchange of surplus goods (e.g. food) for a certain quantity of other goods (e.g. clothing and other apparel), gave way to the introduction of "money" of various types and denominations, or any commodity which was widely acceptable, trading and marketing across geographic frontiers grew rapidly.

At various stages in history, the torch of industrial and economic leadership might be said to have passed from one civilisation to another. The phenomenon of several world industrial leadership phases was highlighted by the Head of Strategic Planning, General Motors Co., on a visit to the Graduate School of Business, University of Chicago. The 1750–1850 British Industrial Revolution phase of leadership could be said to have preceded the 1850–1950 American industrial leadership phase. This led to the question: 1950–2050—who leads? A consensus seemed to forecast Japan/China (in that order), leading possibly to a trans-Pacific/Pacific-rim international marketing network. When India joins those existing and potential industrial leaders, it might be argued that the globe has been truly circled, as some of the earliest traders and international marketers were Indians with their silks and precious stones, to be followed by the Egyptian, Greek, Roman and German Empires, in that order. In fact, those civilisations had their own "freeports" or "free trade zones" in, for example, Venice and Constantinople.

At a time when there was no Concorde or communications satellite, there was a form of international relations cultivated by the early international marketers. Today there is instant communication, travel and transport through rapidly changing global networks, and a return of the concept of international marketing centres such as free trade zones in the United States, and freeports in the United Kingdom and parts of Europe. There are also rapidly expanding free trade zones in various developing countries, and it is estimated that over 20 per cent of world trade will move through these zones by 1990 (*see* Chapter 21). Unfortunately, there is still a threat to world peace, with war in many parts of the world, such as the Middle East and Latin American countries. The emergence of trade blocs, thus increasing localised international marketing, has improved relations between member countries. Examples are the European Economic Community (EEC), and the Association of South-East Asian Nations (ASEAN). While the development of those trade blocs has accelerated *intra*-continental marketing, it might be said that the emergence of multinationals during this century has facilitated *inter*-continental marketing. There is now the increasingly common phenomenon of various machines and parts of a system being manufactured in one continent, and assembled in another, for example (*see also* Appendix III):

(*a*) a computer system is assembled in Ireland, with United States components shipped in by Boeing 747 weekly, and later sold in the German market;

(*b*) Tinkabi tractors are assembled in Swaziland, South Africa, with an Indian engine and exported to Kenya.

Another example of inter-continental marketing is when similar motor cars and production systems are featured under different labels in various countries, e.g. the Vauxhall Cavalier (United Kingdom), Opel Monza (Continental Europe) and the Chevrolet Monza (United States and Brazil).

To facilitate these international marketing initiatives, there has been a growth in international education and language teaching in the latter half of the twentieth century, particularly a trend towards the internationalisation of business education.

GATT AND EEC

The high level of interdependency in international trade has led to the establishment of agencies which will act as a police force to ensure that the rules are not broken. The General Agreement on Tariffs and Trade (GATT) is the best known of these. The European Commission seeks to ensure that free trade exists, at least within defined limits in the EEC. As the level of international marketing increases, so these agencies will play an increasingly important role.

GATT has had some success in reducing national formal tariffs, but appears powerless to deal with national tariff barriers. Many aspiring exporters to Japan report examples of national tariff barriers there, i.e. rules and regulations effectively making it very difficult for exporters to penetrate the Japanese markets. Within the EEC, nationalism has been seen raising its head through national tariff barriers. The following are some frequently quoted examples.

(*a*) The Italians ban a German cheese called Quark, simply because it does not fit into any existing category of acceptable import.

(*b*) Consignments of Danish bacon are held up by French customs officers and French farmers attack Danish lorries on isolated roads.

(*c*) Irish law says that furniture must carry instructions and warning labels in Gaelic which poses horrendous problems for importers who have never heard of Gaelic.

(*d*) The Italians ban imports of apple vinegar because their laws state that vinegar must be made from wine (and there is a great deal of surplus wine in Italy).

(*e*) In Belgium, margarine can only be sold in square tubs. Competing brands from abroad, like Blue Band or Stork, cannot be marketed without costly packaging changes.

OTHER INTERNATIONAL AGENCIES

Much of the growth in international trade and international relations, particularly between the industrialised countries of the "North" and the developing countries of the "South", has been promoted by a range of international agencies, including the following.

(*a*) *The World Bank and the International Monetary Fund*, to assist with financing projects on an international scale. Many Third World countries would otherwise find it difficult to finance major irrigation, agricultural and industrialisation projects.

(*b*) *The United Nations*, with a range of specialist agencies such as the International Trade Centre (ITC) at Geneva, which is devoted to improving export performance of developing countries (*see also* Chapter 4), and the Food and Agriculture Organisation (FAO), with its headquarters in Rome, which assists with a comprehensive range of agricultural development in Third World countries.

(*c*) *The World Health Organisation* (WHO), which exists to develop health care systems and fight disease in many parts of the world.

All these agencies provide vital mechanisms for tackling the scandal of the "North/South" differential in an integrated way. However, there are, in addition, many bilateral schemes which industrialised countries support.

IMPACT ON INDIVIDUAL PEOPLE

In all discussions on large agencies with multi-million-dollar budgets, it is easy to overlook the impact on individual people—whether as workers or consumers—of international marketing. In the industrialised world, individual households have never been more informed of world events and markets, through newspapers, magazines and other media. As consumers they are increasingly aware of the origins of products, and, whether unemployed or in work, of the need for export-led growth to maintain standards of living.

In developing countries, people are either at starvation level, too weak to eat whatever grubs or leaves they can scavenge, or having to cope in five years with change that has taken fifty years in industrialised countries. Swaziland is a typical case in that the transistor at the ear of the cyclist, the colour television in the hotel room and the Royal Swazi jet are juxtaposed with primitive conditions—the airport wooden hut, associated with the days of the Dakota aircraft, and the bicycle rather than cars or a bus service for public transport. However, as long as that transistor (and the inevitable Coca-Cola tin) are evident, there is the certainty that international markets and an increasing awareness of world events are around the corner.

It is interesting to note that so-called isolated populations removed from the main international market networks are now beginning to become conscious of world market opportunities. The current drive in China to open up its culture and to learn about industrialisation and international marketing presages the promise of a future world industrial power of a country with 25 per cent of the world population in its domestic market. The Soviet Bloc and Comecon countries (Eastern European trading bloc) have also been conscious of international trade and its importance in recent years.

MULTI-FACETED IMPACT OF INTERNATIONAL MARKETING

When historians look back at the last quarter of the twentieth century, they are likely to comment on the remarkable pace of change which has characterised it. This pace of change is perhaps more difficult for those enclosed in the time capsule of the "now" to note, but nonetheless, it takes only a moment's reflection to realise that most aspects of our life are touched by a dynamic which has an unseen source but a very evident effect. It is not the purpose of this section to relate how widespread the wind of change is, but it may be useful to look at how people and institutions are likely to be affected in one important area, that of the world market environment.

The United Kingdom faces a radical change in its own patterns of activity within the world market environment. The next few years are likely to reveal a much changed position in relation to markets and products. These changes will affect all levels of society, from the individual to the company, to governments and in turn, international relations.

For historical reasons, trade has had a vital part to play in the United Kingdom's development. The industrial infrastructure as well as financial institutions all reflect the influence of trade. That influence is likely to continue, and hence its importance to every facet of society.

The ability of merchants, military men and politicians to find markets for Britain's new textile mills in the eighteenth century had a strong influence on the shape of social and political institutions. Living standards are still strongly linked to international trade in a country where about 30 per cent of production is exported. The future living standards of the work-force are therefore closely associated with the success or otherwise of attempts to market products overseas. Job security and job creation will be even more closely linked to international trade than before. The employees of a company involved in exporting are faced with change. There is likely to be renewed emphasis on quality and delivery as the company seeks to compete in a foreign market.

The ability to see one's goods in export markets can often depend very much on the strength of home markets. The Japanese have succeeded so well in their international marketing efforts, partly because of the large and well-protected home markets. When operating from a secure home market, the ability to market abroad means increased scales of production, which in turn mean lower unit costs. The lower unit costs will be passed on to the home market, which is strengthened against competition from abroad.

One of the most potent forces involved in the growth of world trade and the importance of international marketing is the fact that companies are becoming less committed to their country of origin, and more influenced by their multinational activities. The growth of multinational companies is likely to continue apace. A number of factors have led to this. The communications revolution has meant that physical distance and to some extent language no longer provide insurmountable problems to companies. The formation of trade blocs such as the EEC has encouraged this as has the easing of restrictions on international transactions of financial resources.

Companies are increasingly looking beyond their home base for not only markets but also manufacturing facilities. The concept of "global companies" is one which has become a reality, even stretching over the East/West barriers. However, not all companies lend themselves to global or international competition. Many have products that differ greatly from country to country, or lack sufficient scale economies to yield the exporter a significant competitive edge.

The decision to go into international marketing is no longer one which can be put off by many companies, particularly those involved in consumer goods, manufacturing, electronics and light engineering. To take this step requires a high degree of strategic planning. The company must ask if it has the resources required before entertaining a global marketing strategy. It must look at its competitors and their products, as well as its own, and finally ask what form of strategic innovation would be required to trigger global competition.

SUMMARY

International marketing is not new, but continues to evolve, and it plays a key role in global unity, global perspective and international relations, at individual as well as company and national level.

Many international agencies play a key role in the development of international trade. The General Agreement on Tariffs and Trade (GATT) is the best known of these. The European Commission also plays an important part in the promotion of European and international trade, against a background of attempts to sustain non-tariff barriers.

In conclusion, it is likely that the remainder of the twentieth century will continue to see a growth in international marketing. Companies seek to survive by exploiting their competitive position in the market. Technology, communications and economies of scale will continue to widen the scope of economic activity beyond national boundaries. The signs are that if there is no move strategically towards global marketing, the competitiveness of British industry will be severely diminished, and then the United Kingdom home market will be undermined and lost.

QUESTIONS

1. From your readings, outline and discuss the possible impact on local people of the decision to set up the Nissan car plant in the north-east of England.

2. Evaluate the role of the United Nations in the promotion of world trade.

CHAPTER THREE

Cultural, Political and Legal Adaptations

OBJECTIVES

World marketing is affected and influenced by cultural, economic and societal factors. The economic status of some countries makes them less or more likely candidates for international business expansion. Certain cultural, economic and societal variables will play a significant role in determining the profitability of an overseas operation.

This chapter aims to provide the reader with an understanding of:

(a) cultural, political and legal adaptations for international marketing; and

(b) how the basic philosophy of a person or a company can change as a result of the international marketing experience.

By adaptation is meant, quite simply, adapting your message to your audience. Carrying this out across a language barrier with promotions material is a special form of adaptation.

CULTURAL CONSIDERATIONS

Of the many forces that bear on buying decisions, culture is perhaps the one most often taken for granted. Cultural values typically come last in the list when considered with economic variables, social class, buyers' idiosyncrasies and so on. This attitude probably stems from a common misconception regarding the relevance of culture to marketing, the consequence of which is almost always lost sales opportunities. While it can always be said that consumers are individuals with different needs, motivation or desires, it is also an established principle that individuals within a culture generally rely on some basic values for all types of decisions—those dealing with consumption as well as others.

For the marketing manager, a knowledge of the consumer's evaluation of products and product claims is essential. Further, his ability to compare the characteristics of a number of national markets results in guidelines for adapting domestic marketing strategies to other countries. It is such adaptation that facilitates successful overseas market expansion.

In *Comparative Marketing Systems*, Talcott Parsons and Seymour Lipset isolated five categories to help identify the relevant national values. For them, cultural patterns can be distinguished by the degree to which people:

(a) are either egalitarian or élitist;

(b) are prone to lay stress on accomplishment or inherited attributes;

(c) expect material or non-material rewards;

(*d*) focus on the distinctiveness of the parts (inventiveness) rather than the general characteristics of the whole (extensiveness); and

(*e*) are orientated towards personal rather than group gain.

The UK marketer, when promoting his wares, must take into account the culture of the individuals he is conducting business with and the country's distribution networks.

National traits of EEC businessmen vary from nation to nation. Henry Deschampneufs describes some as follows: "In Belgium ... there is extreme class-consciousness between the Flemish and Walloons ... business must be conducted at high levels ... In Italy, a good deal of business is conducted in cafés ... The French pride themselves on their logic ... The Dutch are stubborn and non-commital ...". The Germans and Italians love concealing information. In the United States, personal output of energy is regarded as a good thing in its own right. Pragmatic ingenuity is valued and is expected to be applied not only to materialistic problems, but to all problems.

The French retailer has been notoriously slow in adopting such recent innovations as self-service supermarkets and national brands. The French retailing system is highly fragmented, with approximately 60 per cent more retail shops in relation to the population than the United States. Even in the wholesale field, the typical organisation is a small one.

All of Kentucky Fried Chicken's eleven Hong Kong outlets failed within two years. Fried chicken apparently conflicted with the fastidious habits of Hong Kong residents who typically provide hot hand towels with meals.

Religion and culture feature prominently in Middle Eastern states. Marketing planners should be fully aware of these in relation to, for example, restrictions on the roles of women in activities such as driving and business management.

POLITICAL INFLUENCES

Political factors greatly influence international marketing. Many nations try to achieve political objectives through international business activities. Firms operating abroad often end up involved in, or influenced by, international relations. There are two forms of political influence, one which involves the international scene, and the second involving internal issues. An example of international political influences is when South African firms have seen the markets for some of their products dwindle as a result of their government's domestic policies. American companies have been boycotted, burned, bombed and banned by people who object to United States foreign policy.

Internal political influences normally take the form of tariff barriers, i.e. taxes levied against products imported from abroad. Tariffs may be classified as either revenue tariffs or protective tariffs. Revenue tariffs are designed to raise funds for the government, while protective tariffs are designed to raise the retail price of imported products to that of a similar domestic product or higher. In the past, it was believed that a country should protect its "infant" industries by using tariffs to keep out foreign-made products. Some foreign goods would enter, but the addition of a high tariff payment would make domestic products competitive. While the general movement has been towards formal tariff reduction, economic downturns always bring calls for economic protection of domestic industries and their employees, and this has been increasingly in the form of non-tariff barriers. An example is the policy of French Customs towards Japanese videos, when the Customs post was moved to a small village miles away from the frontier, and inaccessible to heavy traffic.

Quotas, embargoes and exchange control are additional means whereby governments can control foreign imports. A quota sets limits on the amount of products in certain categories that may be imported, the objective of which can be to protect local industry, or preserve foreign exchange. The ultimate form of quota is embargo, where there is a complete ban on importing certain products. Foreign trade can also be regulated by exchange controls through a central bank or government agency. Exchange control means that firms gaining foreign exchange by exporting must sell this foreign exchange to the central bank or agency. Importers must buy foreign exchange from the same organisation. The exchange control authority can then allocate, expand or restrict foreign exchange according to existing national policy.

Balance of payments problems have become a matter of critical national concern in most (non-OPEC) countries, in part because of the widening gap between domestic needs and domestically available resources and in part because of the rapid increase in price for critical imports, most notably crude oil. In some less-developed countries, e.g. Turkey and Peru, this balance of payments problem has begun to approach the dimensions of a national economic disaster. In many other countries, e.g. Brazil and Argentina, the concern is no less real.

United Kingdom importers to Spain may encounter substantial delays and difficulties in receiving payment for goods exported. Traditionally, Spanish firms expect three months' credit and even then are notoriously dilatory in actually transferring payments. However, the government does place bureaucratic hindrances on the transfer of cash payments. Furthermore, it is difficult accurately to assess a firm's creditworthiness as company reports and accounts are not automatically filed, and those that are produced are not in any way as complete as those kept in Registration House, London.

In Italy, most distributing firms, including wholesalers, retailers and those in public business, must be licensed by municipal boards before they can operate—a practice introduced by the guild system of the middle ages. The government, particularly at the federal level, is involved in distribution to a much greater extent than in many other western countries. In some Arab countries such as Libya the use of *local* agents is compulsory by law, and in China all imports are bought through government agencies.

LEGAL REQUIREMENTS

The legal environment for United Kingdom firms operating abroad is subject to three major influences:

(*a*) British law;
(*b*) international law;
(*c*) legal requirements of host nations.

In the United Kingom, the Monopolies Commission monitors possible monopolistic trading practices, while in the United States there are anti-trust laws. International marketing is subject to various trade regulations, tax laws and import/export requirements. Some nations have a "local content law" that specifies the portion of a product that must come from domestic sources.

International law can be found in treaties, conventions and agreements that exist between nations. Other international business agreements concern international standards for various products, patents, trade marks, reciprocal tax treaties, export control, international air travel and communications.

Consumers are not very discerning individuals, and consequently are protected in the UK by legislation, e.g. the Trade Descriptions Act, or by bodies such as the Advertising Standards Authority. There are equivalents in many other countries.

A legal requirement world-wide is the health warning on cigarettes. The Canadians see beer advertised on television, but no one is seen drinking it. Commercials for chocolates on Dutch television carry tooth decay warnings. In Australia, New Zealand and South Africa it is a legal requirement that all power tools be equipped with a suppressor to prevent radio and television interference.

CHANGE IN PHILOSOPHY: CASE STUDIES

The following examples show that people and companies can be transformed in the course of ten years of international marketing.

An art graduate in Sri Lanka developed his flair for Batik design, starting in a small way in an old garage with three female workers, providing for the tourist market. Over a number of years, through good design and quality finish, he established a new factory outside Colombo employing 300 workers, and successfully marketed 75 per cent of his products to sophisticated international markets such as the United States, Canada, Scandinavia and West Germany. In his early thirties, this young man has become a sophisticated international marketer, making several successful business trips each year, speaking fluent English, and adapting his own style, approach and design to various cultures. (*See also* Appendix III.)

Another example of international marketing success achieved from modest beginnings was a United Kingdom-based organisation, which saw the need in the Middle East for streamlined farm systems, and met this need by transforming desert land to arable farmland, and providing dairy herds to survive in conditions not thought possible in the 1960s. It is interesting to note how this company has integrated, over a ten-year period, into the local culture, and overcome the barriers of politics, legal requirements and very different value systems. Over 500 people from the British Isles have now adapted to life in these quite different cultures and tough environmental conditions, with temperatures of over 150°F (65°C).

These cases epitomise the adaptability of people and companies to many varied cultures and markets.

SUMMARY

There is considerable variation in marketing practices throughout the world. Cultural, legal, political and other considerations must be taken into account before a firm is to launch a product or marketing campaign in a new country. Aggressive sales efforts may be regarded negatively in some foreign cultures, while in others they are essential. Business customs and traditions may restrict a firm's distribution strategy to certain marketing channels. Product names which are to be marketed internationally must be translated into all languages, for example "mist" seems acceptable in most languages, but in German it means "manure". Bribery, other clandestine pay-offs and sometimes dubious use of sales agents in foreign markets have received considerable publicity in recent years, but in some cultures they are considered normal. To ignore any of these or other considerations could be a formula for marketing failure.

QUESTIONS

1. Select a particular example in your region of a company which has "matured" in international marketing, and assess how this might have changed the company's/business leaders' perspectives.

2. How has the emergence of trade blocs such as the EEC assisted with the lowering of cultural, political and legal barriers within the member countries of the Community?

CHAPTER FOUR

Specialist Agencies

OBJECTIVES

This chapter aims to give the reader a greater understanding of specialist agencies and their approach to the development of international marketing. The international marketer should avail himself of all relevant information and support when attempting to penetrate new markets. Much of this support is available quickly, and sometimes free or at a very reasonable price, depending upon which part of the world the exporter or potential exporter is based. Sources of information and support may be at national or international level, or both. Figure 6 outlines a possible information network. It should be emphasised that government agencies in the target country can also sometimes give valuable advice, especially with regard to import/export statistics and possible sources of competition.

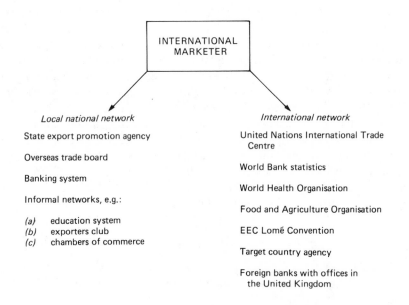

Fig. 6. *Sources of information.*

LOCAL NATIONAL LEVEL SUPPORT

For comparative purposes, it is proposed to examine local support systems in two EEC countries: the United Kingdom (UK) and Ireland.

United Kingdom

In the UK, the British government offers the following services, some of which are free.

(a) The official trade and navigation returns, which indicate details of all exports from and imports into Britain.

(b) The Export Service bulletin, which gives up-to-date details of export opportunities world wide.

(c) Economic surveys which give up-to-the-minute details of local economic conditions.

(d) Commercial officers of the Board of Trade (BoT) stationed overseas, who will feed back information to the BoT on request from a company. They can also be consulted locally by visiting businessmen.

(e) The Department of Trade and Industry (DTI), which operates a computerised export intelligence service, can supply information concerning, for example:

    (i) opportunities for co-operation with overseas manufacturers;

    (ii) market reports;

    (iii) market indicators to new trade opportunities;

    (iv) tariff and import regulation charges;

    (v) reports on the latest economic and trading situations in over 100 countries;

    (vi) international aid and loan agreements; and

    (vii) trade agreements.

(f) The DTI also provides certain free export services, including:

    (i) market assessments to help companies discover where their best export prospects are;

    (ii) up-to-date information on tariff and import regulations, duties and overseas restrictions;

    (iii) overseas business visits services, such as making contacts for UK company executives and assembling information that will be needed to ensure that these visits are effective;

    (iv) the DTI export marketing research advisor who can advise UK companies on whether, and if so how, market research can help with a particular exporting problem, or the most effective method of carrying out the research and commissioning a suitable firm to undertake it;

    (v) the overseas project group, which can help co-ordinate the efforts of British companies with other UK organisations, either in the private or public sector; and

    (vi) advice and help in other ways, when a UK company and its business are affected by the regulations of other countries and international organisations.

Table I which shows the use of resources is taken from the Report of the British Overseas Trade Board (BOTB), 1983. Total net government expenditure, including staff costs and overheads, in support of export

promotion was estimated at £113.5 million for 1983–84, compared with
£90.1 million in 1982–83. (The 1983–84 figure includes some overheads not
included in the 1982–83 figure.) Total allocated resources for the BOTB
and COI (Central Office of Information) for 1983–84 were estimated at
£51.2 million, compared with £48.9 million in 1982–83. (Further information about the BOTB and DTI is given in Chapter 19.)

TABLE I. USE OF RESOURCES IN EXPORT PROMOTION

		£ million	
		1983/84	1982/83
(a)	Collection and dissemination of market intelligence	2.2	2.6
(b)	Trade promotions	18.0	16.5
	of which:		
	Overseas trade fairs (including symposia)	14.7	13.6
	British Export Marketing Centre, Tokyo	—	0.5
	Outward missions	1.8	1.2
	Other	1.5	1.2
(c)	Help to individual exporters	9.1	10.0
	of which:		
	Assistance to capital goods export projects	4.3	5.9
	Export marketing research and advice	1.9	1.0
	Market Entry Guarantee Scheme	1.7	1.4
	Assistance with business visits overseas	1.2	1.7
(d)	Information and publicity directed at overseas markets	10.9	8.7
	of which:		
	Overseas information service	8.9	6.9
	Inward missions and individual business visitors	1.2	1.0
	Other	0.8	0.8
(e)	General advice and financial assistance; support for export promotion services; planning, evaluation and research	11.0	11.1
	Net totals	51.2	48.9

Source: British Overseas Trade Board Report, 1983

British banks are also valuable sources of information. Most of them are
willing to provide:

(a) information on markets and overseas trading conditions;
(b) information regarding tariffs, local taxes and quota restrictions;
(c) advice on desirable methods of payment, foreign exchange, credit
insurance and financing of exports;
(d) status reports on companies and individuals in EEC markets;
(e) advice and assistance on the establishment of subsidiaries, joint

ventures, manufacturing or "know-how" agreements and other business links;

(*f*) advice on documentation and finance of overseas trade generally.

Exporters clubs exist in a number of British cities and these informal organisations provide opportunities to gather advice, facts, opinions and comments about countries from executives of companies actually engaged in trading with them. In some cases, they provide help in selling through a marketing group and/or by organising trade missions and overseas exhibitions. (*See also* Chapter 19.)

Foreign embassies, especially their trade and commercial sections, can provide basic economic and total market information, as well as tariff, quota and trade regulations. They may also provide lists of potential customers, key government agencies, market research and advertising agencies.

Ireland

In Ireland, the Irish Export Board ((*Córas Tráchtála*, or CTT) has "arm's length" distance from the Irish government. This state export board works much more with a private sector style and entrepreneurial flair, although it is still supported by and accountable to the government of Ireland.

CTT also works, probably in a more proactive role, *with* industry rather than *for* industry. There are approximately 250 full-time staff, and a wide range of services is offered in Ireland, and through a network of dynamic overseas offices. Staff are expected to have sector and market specialisations, and probably work more than their UK counterpart *with* the exporter *free of charge*, especially in the initial negotiations with the importer.

The range of services includes:

(*a*) the promotion, assistance and development of export service activities such as architecture, engineering, etc. together with the original export specifications such as agricultural development and processing;

(*b*) construction related, medical and training services;

(*c*) technical and general consulting services, including commercial laboratory services and research and development services;

(*d*) computer software and data processing;

(*e*) public administration and media recording;

(*f*) publishing services.

Over the past twenty-five years the track record of CTT has been very impressive, and this has been recognised internationally. Figure 7 and Table II summarise the very impressive growth of Irish exports, from 1972 to 1982, as shown in the CTT Annual Report 1982.

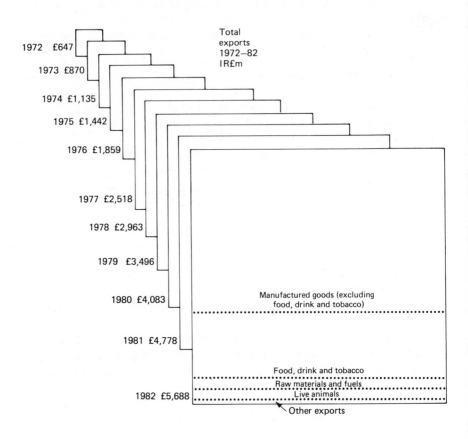

Fig. 7. *Growth of Irish exports, 1972–82.*

TABLE II.   IRISH EXPORTS BY MAIN CATEGORIES
(£ *million*)

	☆Manufactured goods	Food, drink and tobacco	Raw materials and fuels	Live animals	Other exports
1982	3,658	1,535	267	169	59
1981	2,984	1,367	213	168	45
1980	2,391	1,317	208	136	31
1979	1,987	1,163	188	131	27
1978	1,610	1,013	132	180	28
1977	1,384	846	113	153	22
1976	977	665	90	108	19
1975	669	554	79	124	16
1974	596	375	82	72	10
1973	430	291	57	85	7
1972	303	209	43	85	7

☆Excluding food, drink and tobacco
Source: Irish Export Board 31st Annual Report and Accounts 1982.

Many developing countries have modelled their export promotion agencies on the Irish Export Board, and have had their key staff trained in Ireland. CTT works closely with the United Nations International Trade Centre in Geneva, and the EEC Lomé section responsible for assisting Third World exports.

CTT also works closely with the various Irish embassies around the world. Exporters clubs are not as well organised in Ireland as in the United Kingdom. In fact, despite all this enlightened support, indigenous Irish industry still has a long way to go in export development. (*See also* Chapter 19 and Appendix III.)

DEVELOPING COUNTRIES' NATIONAL SUPPORT SYSTEMS

Many developing countries have made international marketing their priority, as this is one way of obtaining scarce foreign currency. Examples included here are Sri Lanka and Thailand.

Sri Lanka
Sri Lanka is an island approximately the size of Ireland with a population of about 15 million (four times that of Ireland). In 1979, the Sri Lanka Export Development Board (EDB) was founded, with representation from the relevant ministries. A wide range of services is available free of charge from the EDB.

In that first year alone (1979), the following were among the trade and investment missions which visited Sri Lanka:

(a) Trade Delegation from Australia (January);
(b) Economic Delegation from Yugoslavia (March);
(c) Agri-business Group from Holland (March);
(d) Romanian Economic and Trade Delegation (April);
(e) India Automobile and Ancillary Industries Delegation (April);
(f) Japan–Sri Lanka Business Co-operation Committee (August);
(g) Delegation from Finland (October);
(h) French Industrial and Economic Mission (Patromat) (November);
(i) Polish Chamber of Foreign Trade Delegation (November);
(j) Mission for European Centre for Industrial Co-operation (CECI) (December).

It is interesting to note that, although Sri Lanka was colonised three times—by the Portuguese from 1500 to 1650; by the Dutch from 1650 to 1800; and by the British from 1800 to 1947—only the Dutch are included in the above list (admittedly only a sample of one year). It should also be noted that the Eastern European countries are well represented in the list, although not normally associated with global international marketing.

Thailand

Thailand has a longer, more impressive track record in export promotion through its Export Promotion Organisation, under the Department of Commercial Relations, Ministry of Commerce. Appendix I contains extracts from *Thailand's Exporters 1980–81*, published by the Thailand Ministry of Commerce. They show the importance and the range and depth of export promotion efforts by a commercially progressive developing country such as Thailand.

THE INTERNATIONAL TRADE CENTRE

The International Trade Centre, in Geneva, Switzerland, is a United Nations agency. Its services are largely free to developing countries, but are often used by other countries at a charge. Although based in Geneva, the ITC has a very impressive network of representatives and contacts around the world in developing countries. Its main objective is to assist developing countries in their export promotion efforts. Market studies are provided for specific products, as well as specific market profiles of countries. In addition to its published studies, the ITC has a trade enquiry service, and supplies computerised trade data for specific products. It also provides a range of other services, including highly specialised consultancy and training services in export policy formulation and implementation, and relevant institutional development. ITC export training materials are used widely throughout developing countries. Two examples which readers would find useful are *Export Product Development* and *Introduction to Export Market Research*.

OTHER SOURCES OF INFORMATION

In carrying out international market investigations, it is vital to use all the available sources of information and support. The following is just a small sample of other institutional organisations which may prove useful.

The European Economic Community

The Community has arrranged preferential agreements with such countries as Israel, Malta, Morocco, Turkey and Switzerland. These agreements provide for the reduction by both contracting parties of barriers to trade over certain goods. Further agreements have been made with the eighteen signatories to the Yaounde Convention, who allow free access to industrial exports within their members. The EEC grants substantial aid to these countries, and has received free access to their markets. A further arrangement, the Arusha Agreement, which has a similar effect to the Yaounde Convention, allows imports from the EEC free of most quantitative restrictions.

Address: The European Economic Community
       200 rue de la Loi
       1049 Brussels

United Nations
The UN publishes statistical series on trade, industry and many other economic aspects, national and international; and special studies on various topics which may be related to market development.

Address: United Nations Sales Section   United Nations Publications
       Palais des Nations   LX2300, United Nations
       1211 Geneva 10   New York, NY 10017
       Switzerland   United States

Food and Agriculture Organisation (FAO)
Statistical series on agriculture and related areas; special studies, including market profiles.

Address: Food and Agriculture Organisation of the United Nations (FAO)
       Distribution and Sales Section
       Via delle Terme di Caracalla
       00100 Rome
       Italy

Organisation for Economic Co-operation and Development (OECD)
Studies and statistical series on foreign trade, industry, science and technology, food, transport, etc.

Address: Organisation for Economic Co-operation and Development
       (OECD)
       Publications Office
       2 rue Andrè Pascal
       75775 Paris, Cedex 16
       France

United Nations Conference on Trade and Development (UNCTAD)
Conference papers and special studies related to many aspects of international trade, such as trade barriers and the Generalised System of Preferences.

Address: UNCTAD
       Palais des Nations
       1211 Geneva 10
       Switzerland

United Nations Economic Commissions
Statistics and special studies related to their respective geographical areas.

Address: United Nations Economic Commission for Europe (EC)
       Palais des Nations
       1211 Geneva 10
       Switzerland

International Monetary Fund

Reports on national and international foreign exchange regulations and other trade barriers, foreign trade and financial and economic developments.

Address: International Monetary Fund
19th and H Street NW
Washington, DC 20431
United States

Most of these organisations issue catalogues or lists of their publications. However, many special reports and other sources of information generated by them are not published and never appear in these lists, but can often be obtained by corresponding directly with the appropriate units of the organisations. The researcher should therefore become familiar with the structure of each of the important organisations and with the type of work undertaken by the various units within them.

SUMMARY

In this chapter, an attempt has been made to emphasise the importance of identifying and using both national and international support systems. National support systems have been compared and some insights given on the extent to which these are being developed in Third World countries. In this context, much may be learned about Thailand's import needs from studying its export documentation, as sources of capital equipment and raw materials can often be a problem.

An outline of various international agencies is also provided. It has been emphasised that many of their services are available free, or at a reasonable charge.

QUESTIONS

1. "A developing country wishing to set up an export promotion agency should be careful of slavishly following the United Kingdom or Irish model." Discuss.

2. Identify a local manufacturer and outline the advice you would give him in using the national and international networks in his export development planning.

CHAPTER FIVE

Approaches to International Market Segmentation

OBJECTIVES

The last four chapters were very much scene-setting for this key chapter which is concerned with selectivity on an organised basis. The more specific the objective or target in any enterprise or endeavour, the more likely the success in accomplishing the task. So it is with international marketing. There is no such entity as "the world market or markets". There are many, many different markets, each quite specific and at different stages of growth and maturity, with very many diverse needs comparatively (inter-market diversity) and within each market (intra-market diversity). The key issue in international marketing is to reconcile the products or services that the business offers with the priority needs of its targeted markets. There may be the "blunderbus" approach, with efforts scattered without much impact anywhere, or the "point 22" approach, with precision impact on precisely defined markets. The latter is to be preferred, but is only feasible on the basis of systematic segmentation of the global market-place, and a screening approach in which target markets are prioritised. In this chapter, therefore, the reader will have the opportunity to analyse the concept of market segmentation and apply it on a global basis, as a preparation for the development of an international marketing strategy discussed in Chapter 6.

THE CONCEPT OF MARKET SEGMENTATION

It is obviously not feasible for any business to serve total markets or the world (markets), except in possibly some unique product or service, or some small specialised market. It is therefore vital, with limited re- sources, for a business leader to segment the market or markets. This market segmentation approach attempts to determine differences between potential buyers in a systematic way (regarding preferences/needs, buying habits, etc.). The rationale is that these differences will impact on the buying decisions, and that the total market is not homogeneous (or similar) in respect to customer preferences and response to products, price, pro- motion or channels of distribution. Examples of these are the type and prices paid for clothing according to income levels of customers. Some buy in street markets and low-priced stores, while other fashion-conscious customers buy in "up-market" stores such as Harrods of London.

Ideally, the basis of segmentation should be to give maximum hetero- geneity (dissimilarity) *between* segments, and complete homogeneity (similarity) *within* each segment. In this way the customer response to the marketing variables (product, price, promotion and place) will vary more between segments than within them. Business leaders need to understand the demand characteristics of each market, and assess the best fit between these and their business resources and capability, choosing the market(s) with the greatest potential.

There are other factors which complicate this process: political and cultural/religious issues. Examples are the approach to developing countries by ex-colonial powers (a British sales manager may not do as well in Sri Lanka as an Irish sales manager), the treatment of women in the Middle East, and the sales of South African goods in other African countries.

The market segmentation approach applies therefore *between* international markets (inter-market) and *within* international markets (intra-market). An example of inter-market segmentation would be that the needs of the German market are very different from the needs of the Nigerian market. Intra-market segmentation is also vital in that within a country, there are very distinct market segments, such as a wealthy market segment in India with its own distinctive needs which are different from the majority of the India market. A further example is that the market in any international city varies from the stockbroker/banker residential belt to the depressed inner city residential area.

Of course, there are many other approaches to market segmentation, for example age groups. Another approach is segmentation in the supply side, for example industrial products (components and equipment for industry or agriculture) and consumer products (home equipment and consumables) and the increasingly important industrial services and consumer services sectors. All of these impact on the market segmentation process.

The basic aim of market segmentation must again be emphasised: to define clearly what it is the business is offering, to whom, and where.

SOME APPLICATIONS OF MARKET SEGMENTATION

Market segmentation and product differentiation are aspects of product policy which sometimes have more applications and potential in domestic marketing, where the firm is trying to develop products or services for various sub-markets to gain a monopolistic or semi-monopolistic position.

However, there are examples of this policy at work in international marketing, where it vies with the standardisation/mass production policy. Examples of the latter include world products such as Coca-Cola, Levi jeans, Wimpey, Xerox, Kodak and Smirnoff Vodka. In the service sector, a company like McDonald's is a good example of standardisation world-wide.

In contrast, the development of multi-grade dispensing pumps for gasoline represented an attempt by the Sun Oil Company to segment the market. Market segmentation is also seen in product differentiation, involving extensive advertising of different brands of an item, sometimes with only slight variation in product but quite distinctive packaging. An example of this is Winston cigarettes, which are manufactured in the United Kingdom, the United States and South America, with slight differences in each area to meet local consumer preferences.

Impressive efforts are made in many developing countries to adapt products to a particular market, say West Germany, rather than just the EEC, and then particular market segments in West Germany in a particular region or city. Examples are batiks and other silk products, high quality craft work and jewellery from Thailand.

GLOBAL MARKET SEGMENTATION: NORTH/SOUTH

The Brandt reports, *North/South—a Programme for Survival*, simply divided the world into the northern industrialised hemisphere and the southern under-developed hemisphere. However, it is possible, and indeed essential, to segment these two hemispheres further in order to examine more closely the various markets and their needs.

The so-called "South" represents the under-developed countries of the world, which include Latin America, the Caribbean, the African states, the Middle East, and Southern Asia, including the Association of South-East Asia Nations (ASEAN). Australia, New Zealand and Japan are excluded (*see* Fig. 4).

It is important to note that this North/South division needs regular review, as there are some very rapidly developing countries in the "South". For example, Brazil has overtaken the United Kingdom in the world car production league. There are also countries in the "North" not too far from the "South's" most affluent countries, i.e. there is a grey area which includes relatively rich Middle East countries.

MARKET SEGMENTATION OF THE NORTH: INDUSTRIALISED COUNTRIES

There are significant differences between various trade blocs and individual countries within these trade blocs. North America and Canada are regarded as sophisticated markets in both consumer goods and services, and in industrial products and services. Many exporters now consider using the network of free trade zones as marketing and distribution centres.

Although the European Economic Community appears to have been in existence for a lifetime, for many people it is still a collection of quite disparate markets, cultures and languages. The realisation of a United States of Europe is still some way off. Some international marketers argue that there are certain markets more "open" to international trade than others, e.g. Holland, West Germany and Belgium. Following this argument, the new exporter might proceed along a learning curve of more "open" markets first, taking on the more challenging markets such as France after some experience has been gained elsewhere. This approach will, of course, vary across various industries and products.

The Australian and New Zealand markets are often useful targets for exporters from Thailand and other Asian countries.

MARKET SEGMENTATION OF THE SOUTH: DEVELOPING COUNTRIES

As has been shown, there are a wide range of developing countries across the three continents of South America, Africa and Asia. Included in this range are the rapidly developing markets of South Korea, Taiwan, Singapore, Hong Kong and Thailand in Asia, Nigeria in Africa, and Mexico and Brazil in South America. In a special category are the oil-rich Middle East markets, including Saudi Arabia and Libya, with an emphasis on intensive schemes of agricultural, industrial, health and educational development. These present opportunities for United Kingdom, West German and United States "turn-key" tenders, such as the complete design of farm systems projects, hospitals and university development. They also provide work opportunities for semi-skilled workers from Asian countries such as India.

The needs of these more affluent markets, therefore, range across the spectrum of products and systems for agriculture, and industrial and social development schemes, together with quality consumer products such as Rolls Royce cars for parents and sports cars for children. A United Kingdom-based producer of a child's racing car retailing at £2,500 found a strong demand from oil-rich families in the Middle East.

In contrast, the remaining lesser-developed countries are often at subsistence level in terms of food, health care and shelter. The market need is there, but there is the absence of the ability to pay which turns need into the traditional definition of "economic demand". In addition, there is a real need to assist with the most basic and fundamental survival schemes, such as village water/irrigation projects. Water is often, with food, the prime need in the attempt to cope with starvation. Very basic tools and farming and fishing systems for food provision are required. Short-term emergency schemes for food and health survival need to be supported with a self-help approach at village/community level. The often-quoted maxim of today is: "give a man a fish, and you feed him for a day; teach him how to fish, and you feed him for the rest of his life".

There are many funding agencies for the least-developed countries, e.g. the United Nations agencies, Food and Agriculture Organisation, World Health Organisation, World Bank, and EEC Lomé Convention scheme and many bilateral schemes for individual countries. Such schemes constitute market opportunities through a tendering system organised by these third party agencies. However, it should be emphasised that there is still totally inadequate funding provision. This is poignantly seen in that thousands die each day of starvation and disease on one side of the global village, while on the other side, millions die of overeating, attend health farms and organise clandestine disposal of waste and over-production such as milk "lakes" and butter and meat "mountains". The term "village" is an appropriate metaphor, as a result of instant communication through satellite television. Thus the affluent 20 per cent of the world's population do know fully of the millions of their starving brothers and sisters. Their shame has its location on all three continents: South America, Africa and Asia.

SOVIET UNION AND THE COMECON COUNTRIES

The Soviet Union and the Comecon countries of Eastern Europe have their own market needs, and although self-sufficiency and intra-trading feature in their policies, there is an increasing involvement in international trade with European, United States and Third World countries.

In terms of their imports, there is an increasing interest in productivity, computer systems and technology.

Shrewd Third World countries "court" Soviet and United States support, and benefit from a competitive spirit to supply projects and public amenities, often in kind rather than in cash. This is particularly true in some Asian Third World countries. Exporting to East European countries means a need to develop a trusting relationship with the state buying agency. Buying procedures and documentation are detailed and time-tabled, although once the tender is chosen, payment is assured and is strictly according to the agreed timetable.

JAPAN AND CHINA

Japan

The Japanese are noted for one of the most professional approaches to international marketing. Jetro is the state export agency, and the partnership between state and private sector is a feature of their legendary success in world markets.

Another policy they adopt is the local "cascade" approach, whereby they pass on their know-how and technology "mark I" to satellite countries such as South Korea and Taiwan, while they move into second and third generation technologies. This has the effect of promoting prosperity and purchasing power in neighbouring countries, thereby providing local export markets for products of their advanced technologies.

The international image is one of product quality and professionalism. The Chairman of Sony commented at a recent conference that in the late 1940s and early 1950s, the words "made in Japan" were printed as small as possible, because of the poor quality image. Now thirty years later these same words are in bold lettering—a complete transformation within a single generation.

Japan as a target market for exporters has the reputation for non-tariff barriers (*see* Chapter 3). This is a really difficult penetration challenge, but professional international marketers have shown that it is possible to overcome these problems.

China

China is one country that has captured the imagination of many international marketers. Many would describe it as a slumbering giant, with one-quarter of the world's population, a diligent, intelligent people with deep resolve. The national resources of that vast land have not been exploited, and some commentators predict that it will be the leading world industrial power in the first half of the twenty-first century.

Interestingly, China has recently been keen to study western knowledge in terms of industrial organisation, technology and marketing. The government of China is now developing, with EEC assistance and methodology, its first business school project (1984–89), with targets of nearly 100 Master of Business Administration (MBA) graduates in the first five years.

China should present interesting possibilities in the next decade of agricultural and industrial revolution for international marketers, accompanied by predictable health, education and infrastructure development schemes.

SUMMARY

The essence of this chapter is a panoramic view of the global market-place, with market opportunities available according to the stage of development of the various regions outlined above. It is this variety of opportunity and challenge that constitutes the adventure and excitement of international marketing.

QUESTIONS

1. As a producer of textile machinery, how would you analyse international marketing opportunities?

2. You are requested as a graduate consultant to advise a producer of dairy products on identification and screening of potential world markets. Discuss your approach.

CHAPTER SIX

Development of an International Marketing Strategy

OBJECTIVES

In many cases firms "stumble" into international marketing without a coherent policy and plan. It may arise from a chance enquiry, or a random meeting at an exhibition, or a desperate effort to bridge a period of difficulty in the home market. Success in international marketing is more likely when a basic strategy has been developed, consistent with the overall corporate strategy and in the context of existing or potential capability—managerial, marketing, technical/product and financial. This chapter aims to give the reader an insight into some of the key questions and approaches to the formulation of an international marketing strategy for a particular firm.

INTERNATIONAL MARKETING STRATEGY IN CONTEXT

It is essential that international marketing strategy be consistent with:

(a) the firm's marketing strategy; and
(b) the overall corporate strategy of the business.

Corporate strategy is assumed to evolve from the interaction of the three components shown in Fig. 8, part (a). Marketing strategy and international marketing are shown as subsets of this strategy in part (b).

The corporate strategy model outlined in Fig. 8 needs much further development, especially as regards introducing a *dynamic*. The external scene changes very rapidly, and the changes are often lurches rather than gradual, for example the emergence of new technologies, rapid market movements and changes in competitive positions with sudden liquidations and new venture formations. When the dynamic is incorporated, we have what is known as "strategic management". This involves a multi-strategy approach to possibly three or four different scenarios. This "what if" approach, which is facilitated by computer systems and software, can give a business the opportunity to assess the impact of various rapid changes, and may lead to a greater state of readiness in the organisation to cope with rapid change. In earlier times, when industries like photography took over a hundred years to evolve, business organisation had little problem in organising accordingly. Today, however, in microelectronic systems and other high technology fields, rapid change is almost continuous and the making/change phase is often six months rather than a hundred years.

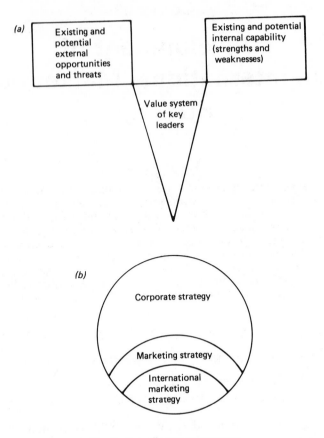

Fig. 8. *Overall corporate strategy.*

It is obvious from this outline approach to strategic management that marketing, and particularly international marketing, must be even more prepared for, and must indeed search out, environmental change and all its implications.

Even for the smaller and medium-sized firm, some simple questions can be put in terms of the business and its owners, e.g. the following.

(*a*) Where are we now?
(*b*) How did we get here?
(*c*) Where are we going? Why?
(*d*) Where else could we go? Why?
(*e*) Where should we go?
(*f*) How? What is to be done?
(*g*) Who is to do it?
(*h*) Where and when is it to be done?

Such systematic planning needs regular, sometimes annual review, as shown in Fig. 9. All these questions and the particular framework can be applied to the marketing and international marketing planning framework to be discussed later in this chapter.

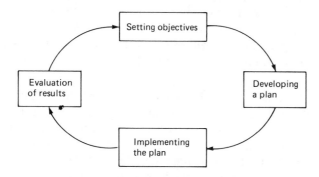

Fig. 9. *Systematic planning and review.*

RATIONALE FOR GOING INTERNATIONAL

The question of motivation for international marketing can be examined from different perspectives:

(*a*) the business owner and his business;
(*b*) the physical locality of the business;
(*c*) the local industry or sector setting; and
(*d*) the government of the country (national economic perspective).

Many analysts start with the last perspective—the national economic perspective—but it is important to remember that it is the businessman who makes the decision to go international, and although there is obviously a sense of patriotism, it is essentially a personal and company-motivated decision.

As mentioned earlier, it is unfortunate that many initial international marketing decisions are not thought out, with consequent failure. They arise from a chance meeting on vacation, or a letter of enquiry or a panic effort to cope with competitive market conditions at home, often connected with a domestic sales slump. There is usually no time to plan, and the action taken is often damned by low or limited cash funding.

From the businessman's point of view
The following are some reasons why international marketing might make sense from the businessman's point of view.

(*a*) *More stability.* Where the home market is of limited size, for example a small country with limited purchasing power, or an island economy, other markets provide a broader and possibly more stable base. This is particularly important in times of economic recession, as in general

not all markets will trough at the same time, or recover at the same time.
  Demand may also have the following limitations in the domestic market:
    (*i*) seasonality of goods for climatic reasons; examples are summer
wear and rainwear (umbrellas);
    (*ii*) seasonal demand owing to religious or cultural mores; examples
are Christian feast periods, and Buddhist and Moslem religious festivals.
  Sales in export markets will often fill the "troughs" in demand. Thus
factories are kept busy throughout the year, and cash flow problems are
eased.

  (*b*) *Lower unit costs.* Businessmen sometimes believe that exports will
be unprofitable because of higher marketing expenses and lower prices.
However, this is not always the case, since with modern distribution
systems, the economics of transportation, and an international network of
freeports or free trade zones, the international marketing process can be
very streamlined. In addition, the higher volume and plant utilisation can
often mean lower unit costs, yielding overall greater profits.

  (*c*) *Access to foreign exchange.* In many countries, particularly developing countries, only exporting companies are allowed foreign exchange
(which is often a scarce commodity) to buy imported machinery and raw
materials, thus gaining greater flexibility and competitiveness compared
with other local companies.

  (*d*) *New ideas.* In many cases, it is only when a company has to compete
in world markets and is exposed to new ideas from these markets that it
really "comes of age". Such experiences and ideas will improve all aspects
of the company's operations. The development of products for more
sophisticated markets often improves the home market performance. An
example is Jaguar's experience in the United States and West German
markets.

  (*e*) *Personal satisfaction.* From a personal point of view, most international marketers, while emphasising the challenge and hard work, will
suggest it is more exhilarating, more interesting and more enjoyable to
travel and work in the international business environment, rather than to
be confined to the often narrower and unstimulating activities of a staid
home market. In fact, many owners in developing countries admit that it
was only after going international that they fully understood the marketing
process.

From the point of view of the locality/community of the business
There are many advantages to the home community of the exporter,
including:

  (*a*) greater employment opportunities for production and service
workers with a more stable company;
  (*b*) opportunities for travel for key sales staff;

(*c*) possibilities for increased business for local service agencies such as banking, insurance, freight and travel agents;

(*d*) possibilities for greater contact with other nationalities—overseas buyers, visits, international links and twinning between towns and schools with overseas counterparts.

Local industry or sector setting

International marketing by member companies can mean technical and process innovation for an industrial sector. This also means updated know-how, and product adaptation and development. A further advantage will be the lessening of fluctuations in local sales, either seasonal or local cyclical recession for members.

Government/national economic point of view

A high proportion of firms with thriving international marketing action plans will:

(*a*) ensure foreign currency which can be used to purchase imports;
(*b*) assist with national balance of payments surplus or deficit;
(*c*) lead to better use of national resources;
(*d*) help to ease local recessions and unemployment;
(*e*) assist with national development plans and standards of living; and
(*f*) ensure a more outward-looking and updated business community.

FRAMEWORK FOR DEVELOPING AN INTERNATIONAL MARKETING STRATEGY

Any international marketing strategy should be consistent with the overall corporate strategy and marketing plans of the company. The development of an international marketing strategy is only one stage in the international marketing process. The strategy will involve the following.

(*a*) *Situational analysis.*
    (*i*) What markets are we in now, with what products?
    (*ii*) How did we reach this position?
    (*iii*) Where are our present plans taking us?
    (*iv*) Why are we going there?
    (*v*) What other market(s) could we be moving into?
    (*vi*) Why these markets?

Figure 10 shows the forces, controllable and uncontrollable, which must be taken into account.

(*b*) *Developing international marketing objectives.*
    (*i*) What markets should we be in?
    (*ii*) With what products, and to what extent?

(*c*) *Formulating the international marketing plans.* How? Who? Where? When? (Integrating market plans with product plans.)

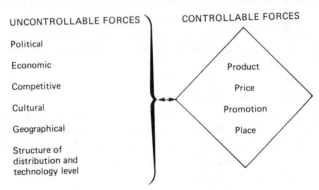

UNCONTROLLABLE FORCES

Political

Economic

Competitive

Cultural

Geographical

Structure of
distribution and
technology level

CONTROLLABLE FORCES

Product

Price

Promotion

Place

Fig. 10. *Forces affecting marketing.*

(*d*) *Implementing the international marketing plans.* Communication and co-ordination:

Main tasks

Managing existing international markets	New international market development
Existing product penetration	Existing product "fit"/adaptation
New product—identification of possibilities	New product possibilities

(*e*) *Evaluation of international marketing process.*

(*f*) *Reformulation of revised international marketing strategy.*

International marketing strategy *development* is essentially concerned with (*a*), (*b*), (*e*) and (*f*) above.

For the company which is going international for the first time, developing a strategy is rooted in good situational analysis and capability appraisal, together with examination of the rationale for wanting to go international. For such a company, the strategy might be to consider, in the first instance, one or two markets where existing or easily adapted products will meet identified needs. The selection or screening of markets is important, as some are more easily penetrated than others, for the following reasons.

(*a*) Greater need and product compatibility.

(*b*) More "open" to importing, with fewer barriers such as language or national mores. For example, some exporters have come of age on a learning curve, including, in order of ease of penetration:

(*i*) year 1—Holland;

(*ii*) year 3—West Germany;

(*iii*) year 5—France.

(*c*) Geographical/cultural closeness.

In summary, international marketing strategy for the initiated might well be based on:

(*a*) lowest risk (lowest cost, greatest knowledge contact);

(*b*) fewer/lower barriers; and

(*c*) selection of one or two markets, and professional planning.

International marketing strategy should also spell out that there is an objective to contribute to a targeted percentage of sales on a three-year planning basis. This should link to the production capability. Is there a 30 per cent or 40 per cent slack? Or is there the financial and management depth for expansion of production capability? For the existing exporter, developing international marketing strategy should include decision-making on whether to:

(*a*) expand in existing overseas markets with existing products or new products;

(*b*) develop new markets with existing or adapted products or new products;

(*c*) withdraw from existing markets;

(*d*) some combination of (*a*), (*b*) or (*c*).

An even more fundamental consideration is whether to increase or reduce the firm's overall commitment to the overseas markets, rather than the domestic market.

In developing an international marketing strategy, there are, therefore, several tensions to be resolved, as follows.

(*a*) How much effort for domestic market and how much for overseas markets?

(*b*) Product standardisation approach for selected "competitive" markets, *or* product differentiation/adaptation for various international markets, *or* key market/segment concentration for just one or two markets?

(*c*) Which approach to use in overseas markets:

    (*i*) selling through intermediaries based in the home market;

    (*ii*) appointment of an agent in the foreign market;

    (*iii*) direct selling by the firm's own representative;

    (*iv*) establishing a marketing/sales subsidiary?

WHAT MARKETS/PRODUCTS AND WHY?

Selecting markets can be one of the most difficult tasks. A good rule is that if you only want two, you should still screen five or six. Just as products have life cycles, so also have markets, with the same phases of development, growth, maturity and decline. In world terms, Bangladesh and Nepal might figure at the lowest end of the development phase, where agricultural development is still in process, where the United States, the United Kingdom and others may be at the end of maturity, or even starting a decline/saturation for some products (*see* Fig. 5, p.9).

In many cases, the firm will often seek markets for its existing product range.

A standard product saleable in many markets without adaptation favours large market numbers, while a product requiring modification to local markets favours concentration. The technology of the product may be important; high technology products may be best marketed world-wide, before substitutes appear, while on the other hand, a new product in short supply may be restricted to a few markets. These points are superseded by the importance of product concentration and specialisation as mentioned earlier. For the specialised product aimed at a small market segment is all but irrelevant, what matters is the world market.

Other factors include the existence of barriers to market entry in some areas, market stability in others and a disproportionately high level of competition in major markets. A final point on this is whether the balance of product and market factors tends to favour exporting to many markets or concentrating on a small number.

SUMMARY

Any international marketing strategy must be developed in the context of the total corporate plan and marketing strategy. For firms about to enter international marketing, understanding *their* rationale is important, as well as careful planning and market/product selection. For existing international marketers, taking stock of the past and present is important before designing plans for the future. Coping with the tension between market concentration and new market development can be a challenge.

QUESTIONS

1. Your advice is needed by an existing exporter. Outline the discussion points for helping with the development of an international marketing strategy.

2. Discuss the advantages of going international in marketing.

CHAPTER SEVEN

Preparing an Export Plan

OBJECTIVES

This chapter aims to set out an export planning framework which the reader should be able to adapt to a modest scale of international marketing operations in a medium-sized company. Any export plan should be based on an international marketing strategy and objectives (*see* Chapter 6). It is important to note that it is the overall export plan in relation to the total business market plan, and not the detailed individual country export plan, which is investigated at this stage. The various components of the export plan, from both a specific market and product type point of view, will be dealt with in later chapters.

PLANNING FOR EXPORTS AGAINST AN AGREED STRATEGY AND OBJECTIVES

The company's international marketing strategy and objectives will be fundamental to the preparation of an export plan. Other key factors affecting the design of the plan include:

(*a*) the types of markets (industrialised, developing, least developed, or others such as Soviet, Comecon, etc.);

(*b*) the types of products (industrial products such as production machinery or components for agricultural or manufacturing processes as distinct from goods);

(*c*) the specific profile of the selected markets; and

(*d*) the competition.

The company must define its export marketing objectives and policies, which will involve the following decisions.

(*a*) What proportion of total sales shall consist of export sales?

(*b*) Shall the company aim for market concentration (a few export markets) or market diversification (several markets each on a smaller scale)?

(*c*) What types of countries shall the company export to, e.g. under-developed nations, oil-producing nations, etc. (as mentioned earlier)?

The degree to which various companies are committed to international marketing will affect their strategy, objectives and export planning. In the early stages of international marketing involvement, the firm may be *ethnocentric* in philosophy (overseas markets are viewed as secondary to domestic markets, primarily used as means of disposing of a surplus of domestic production). However, many firms evolve to the *polycentric* stage, where subsidiaries are established in overseas markets and marketing activities are organised on a country-by-country basis, involving local nationals. In the *regiocentric* and *geocentric* phases, the firm views the region (e.g. the ASEAN region) or the world as a potential market, ignoring national boundaries.

One other aspect of international marketing strategy which will impact on developing export plans is the extent to which the *primary* objective, especially in early years, is to gain market share (as in many Japanese firms for the first five years) or rate of return, as in many United States corporations (*see also* Chapter 18). There is little doubt that Tokyo is also interested in rate of return after the first five years with successful market penetration.

The first stage is to identify potential markets overseas—the company must ensure it knows its markets well. A certain amount of information must be compiled for proper assessment of each market. From an economic standpoint, economies may be classified according to industrial structure, and according to national incomes. Nations also differ greatly in their politico-legal environment in respect to imports and foreign investment. Factors such as attitudes to international buying, political stability, mmentary regulations and government bureaucracy must be assessed. Each country's cultural traditions, preferences and taboos must also be studied. As for distribution, the trading pattern, methods of distribution and any changes taking place must be assessed for each country.

After developing a list of possible countries in which to market, the company must screen and rank them. The core of the ranking procedure is to try to determine the probable rate of return in each market. Kotler lists five steps in the procedure, as follows:

(*a*) estimate of current market potential;
(*b*) forecast of future market potential;
(*c*) forecast of market share;
(*d*) forecast of costs and profits;
(*e*) estimate of rate of return.

At this stage a firm choice or choices will be made, probably after some field research is undertaken to confirm the rankings.

It is now possible for the company to work out its manufacturing and selling strategies for export trading. Basically, there are four options, as outlined below.

(*a*) Manufacture and sell the product from the domestic base. The product may be sold either direct to the customer or by the deployment of some form of intermediary to sell the goods locally.

(*b*) Manufacture but not sell for export, i.e. experts in export marketing handle the selling.

(*c*) Supply skills for others to export, i.e. license others to manufacture and sell in return for royalties on sales made as well as the sale of local manufacturing rights.

(*d*) Manufacture and sell the product from an overseas base, i.e. establish subsidiaries abroad, or a joint venture.

Because of political factors, the company will seldom be able to adopt the same strategy for all demand markets and more than one strategy may have to be adopted according to where the market exists, e.g. it may be necessary to manufacture locally where direct imports are forbidden.

ROLE AND OUTLINE OF THE EXPORT PLANNING FRAMEWORK

The role of the framework is mainly to link up an action plan(s) to the international marketing strategy and objectives. The framework shows an integrated approach in sequence on the "how, where, when, who" questions of implementing the strategy and meeting the objectives. The fact that it is a framework means that there is flexibility for adaptation for various exporting businesses at different stages of involvement in exporting.

As mentioned earlier, there are many factors affecting the preparation of an export plan. However, it may be useful at this stage to consider an outline planning framework in sequence (*see* Fig. 11). It may be seen from the framework that the preparation of the export plan is the bridgehead to action for the international marketing strategy phase. It also constitutes an integrated action plan for overseas market needs satisfaction, and the key area of production capability requisition and mobilisation, culminating in export product development plans.

On completion of the implementation phase, including sales and after-sales service, there are two feedback loops: the micro, or individual customer reaction, and the macro, overall market penetration performance, at $G1$ and $G2$. It is then that a second phase is possible involving a screening and reformulation of strategy at $C2$ (as distinct from phase $C1$).

FACTORS AFFECTING THE EXPORT PLAN FORMULATION

One of the first factors to impact on the formulation of the export plan is the extent of the business's experience of, and its degree of commitment to, exporting. As mentioned earlier, a company "dipping its toe" into export waters for the first time is obviously going to consider a modest export plan—perhaps an existing product with minimum adaptation needs, to be offered in a convenient and accessible export market. Examples would be the Irish market for Northern Ireland companies, or vice versa, and the South India market for a Sri Lanka company, or vice versa. Cultural links and some compatibility are obvious in these instances. However, a more complex export plan is likely to be required when a

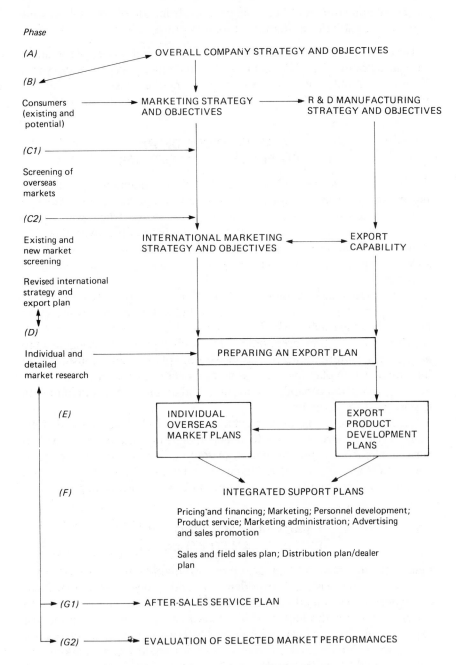

Fig. 11. *Outline export planning framework.*

company has many diverse overseas markets, e.g. a Japanese company selling in Europe, the United States and Asian markets where product adaptation and packaging needs differ for various cultures. In such companies exports might be as high as 80 per cent of sales and constitute the life blood of the business. Another example over the past ten years is the Irish Dairy Board (Bord Bainne), with exports to over eighty markets, and product and marketing adaptations to various cultural and climatic requirements.

Export marketing plans must also take account of the various industrialised systems, Soviet/Comecon and Western industrialised, least developed and developing countries, in terms of state involvement in national procurement, important and attitudes to overseas suppliers. There have been many instances of a slow build-up of relationship and trust with Comecon countries before exporting orders emerge. World Bank, United Nations or EEC financing may be a feature of export planning for Third World countries. The need to overcome non-tariff barriers might well be a feature of plans for exporting to Japan.

Another factor to affect export planning is whether the field is industrial products, consumer products or services, or a combination, e.g. overseas "turn-key" operations. An example of the latter is the design, building and contract management of higher education institutions in Nigeria by a United Kingdom consortium, or the design, development and management (including training) of dairy farms, including herd provision/breeding and equipment/farms systems supply, in the Middle East by a Northern Ireland company. Another complex exporting plan is the multi-million dollar Mahawelli Dam scheme in Sri Lanka.

The degree to which keen competition and the existence of infratructure and support agency facilities exist in the host as well as the domestic country will also affect the development of export plans.

SCOPE FOR FLEXIBILITY IN EXPORT PLANNING

In the rapidly changing world of the 1980s and 1990s, flexibility must be a key feature of export planning, in terms of technological, social and political change. A current example is the extension of satellite television, which will literally open up markets across national frontiers in terms of a possible marketing communications revolution. How might this contribute to the standardisation of tastes and products across cultural and national frontiers? One example is cable television, and the opening up of United Kingdom television channels to Belgium (which has already caused a boom for snooker and darts equipment in the Belgian market).

As regards social and political change, how might the emergence of trade blocs, more international travel and concepts such as "the United States of Europe" produce a European taste in terms of a possible blurring of national and social norms?

The growth of international trade and further development of an international network of freeports or free trade zones can lead to intensified and sudden competition from developing as well as developed countries. Once again this will mean that export planning will have to be continuously reviewed, and flexibly designed.

REVISION OF THE EXPORT PLAN

Although the export plan should be continuously monitored, a formal review will need to be undertaken at regular intervals, probably once a year. This review should relate back to the original objective and performance, including errors of omission and commission. Care should be taken to monitor and update changes in the various markets, technological updating of products and new potential in terms of both market penetration and new market development. Factors exogenous to the firm must also be evaluated, e.g. the competition and changes in government support schemes in both host and domestic countries. The revised export plan might even need to be based on revised objectives, as the company may wish to be more international. This might include the setting up of subsidiaries in host countries or other modes of deeper involvement, such as joint ventures.

SUMMARY

An outline framework is important to make explicit the various facets of the export plan. The content of that framework is the strategy and overall objectives of the company and its marketing function. Various factors affect the development of the export plan, and the need for flexible planning is essential. A fundamental review of the export plan should be undertaken at regular intervals, ideally once a year.

QUESTIONS

1. As a businessman employing fifty employees, outline the questions and factors you would consider in drawing up your first export plan.

2. A local businessman has asked you as a recent graduate to assist him with a comprehensive revision of his export plan. Discuss the approach you would use.

CHAPTER EIGHT

Market Penetration Tactics

OBJECTIVES

This chapter deals with implementation of the export marketing plan after the international marketing strategy has been formulated. The reader is introduced to an outline of market penetration approaches and particular penetration systems. Broad definitions and approaches are discussed as more detailed treatment is given to elements of the plan in later chapters.

The reader could easily fall into the trap of discussing endless tactics on promotion advertising, selling, etc. There are probably as many tactics as there are salesmen. However, such a treatment of the topic would be akin to the myopic thinking of many firms, particularly those who have disappeared or are about to. The type of thinking referred to is that which concentrates on short-term mechanistic approaches to "selling" rather than effective "marketing".

TACTICS AND STRATEGIES

"Tactic" might be defined as a procedure or device for gaining some end. Tacticians, who may be endowed with great skill and Machiavellian guile, will usually come up with some method of achieving their own particular end, but the important question is whether these ends and methods are in accord with the overall marketing strategy of the firm; in fact, does the firm even *have* an overall marketing strategy?

Michael J. Baker provides a useful definition which, at the same time, describes the difference between, and indicates the interdependence of, strategy and tactics: "In essence, a strategy is a broad statement of the means to be employed in achieving a given objective, while the actual methods used constitute the tactics" (*Marketing—An Introductory Text*).

International marketing strategies vary according to the domestic origin, the company itself and its industry, and of course the particular target market and the state of competition. Tactics for the penetration of these international markets will also vary with strategy related to the above factors.

An example of alternative approaches was discussed in some American research undertaken by a team from the Colombia School of Business into a number of subsidiaries from Japanese, European and United States parent companies, which were located in Brazil. One of the many findings was that the Japanese have a longer-term strategy designed to gain an impressive market share, particularly in the first five years, and then later to acquire the rate of return needed to be accounted for in Tokyo. However, the United States firms had to give a rate of return performance from year 1—a much more immediate return on investment. (*See also* Chapter 18.)

Obviously these two contrasting firms would have very different sets of tactics for penetrating the market. The Japanese subsidiary would tend to emphasise keener pricing and more costly and aggressive promotion tactics in the first few years to gain maximum sales and market share. However, the United States company marketing director would have to achieve the targeted rate of return, and therefore ensure that prices were adequate and that promotion and other marketing costs were strictly controlled, in order that overall costs allowed for the strict target of profit at the specified rate of return.

SALES OR MARKETING?

If market penetration is left to the salesmen, the chances are that the approach will be to "get in there first" and go for a "quick kill". This approach is perhaps understandable from people trained in sales only, whose earnings depend on commission, and who probably know little or nothing of the firm's long-term objectives or strategies.

In his article "From Sales Obsession to Marketing Effectiveness" in the *Harvard Business Review*, Philip Kotler says:

> We tend to confuse marketing effectiveness with sales effectiveness. This is our big mistake—and in the end it hurts sales as well as marketing. A company or division may have a top notch sales force that could not perform better, but if the salesmen don't have the right products to sell, know the best customers and have the best values to offer, their energy counts for little.

So, market penetration tactics, like all other marketing tactics, should be decided upon in the light of the firm's strategy, which has been arrived at after examination of the external and internal realities and the allocation of resources to take advantage of opportunities and deal with threats, in order to achieve specified objectives.

Theodore Levitt, *Innovation in Marketing*, says: ". . . everything a company does—in marketing and everything else—has to be unifying and centripetal, not fragmenting and centrifugal. This requires total overall corporate planning and co-ordination." He argues that the "better mouse-trap" approach to getting and keeping customers is naïve and short-lived and that firms should be addressing the problem of achieving a truly customer-oriented approach. This depends on many factors, including proper analysis of the market and identification of customer needs; properly handled, timely communication with customers; and the establishment of a consistent, genuine and recognisable corporate identity.

An example of customer-oriented approach in international marketing was Marks and Spencer, when they belatedly adapted to French buying behaviour in their Paris stores. This involved changing their store layout, colour scheme and image to allow for changing rooms, which was totally at odds with their British store policy.

Consistency, genuine product and recognisable corporate identity is exemplified by McDonald's food chain in their international marketing performance.

SHORT-TERM/LONG-TERM

If short-term tactics are always to complement the long-run strategies of the firm, then those strategies must be clearly defined to all concerned, not just "key" personnel. If the formulation of corporate strategy can be arrived at in a "bottom-up" manner, involving the lower echelons, so much the better. This should foster a feeling of "ownership" of the plan through-out the firm and ensure a greater commitment to it. Relating this point to market penetration tactics, it would mean that, for example, if the strategy of the firm is to achieve penetration by presenting a quality image, salesmen who identify with the strategy are unlikely to tarnish that image by sloppiness of dress or speech, or poor presentation of the goods or services.

Fig. 12. *Short-term and long-term tactics.*

An example of short- and long-term image building is the quality image of Japanese products. There would appear to be some mismatch between the short-term goals of some Japanese exporters and their longer-term strategy. However, offering quality products at keen prices is still good business sense, when one considers that the overall aim is profitable international trading.

The example in Fig. 12 shows a gradual approach to profitability built on effective promotion of an image of quality and value.

CUSTOMER ORIENTATION

The formulation of the corporate strategy should involve a rigorous examination of all aspects of the firm's existence, and this can be a traumatic experience. The firm must examine its competence in all areas (e.g. production, marketing, management, R and D, etc.). It must examine its history and its image. It must be prepared to redefine what business it is in. It must examine the competition. It must examine the needs and wants, the problems and preferences, the tastes and expectations of its customers.

The strategy must be customer oriented. It must utilise the firm's resources to achieve customer satisfaction, because therein lies longevity and profitability. Adam Smith said: "the interest of the dealers ... is always in some respects different from, and even opposite to that of the public" (*Wealth of Nations*). Levitt says that the attraction and retention of customers depends on the firm reducing the "natural residual of buyer discontent" by "raising the positive element of clear-cut satisfaction". The firm's approach to tactics in market penetration, market development, product development or diversification must, therefore, always be mindful of the need to maintain continuing customer satisfaction.

In international marketing, customer satisfaction is often a weak point when delivery dates and standards of packing and quality control are not adhered to. Successful international market penetration can only be maintained with a first-class distribution and after-sales service. It is essential to get these logistics sorted out in the first instance, build up a reputation for reliability, and then maintain that reputation. This whole area of customer service demands much attention and capital investment, particularly in the motor car industry. This proved to be a key question for United States customers and agents when the new De Lorean car was produced in Northern Ireland for the United States market.

WORK-FORCE AND AGENTS' EDUCATION AND TRAINING

Simon Majaro says that the first task in the development of an effective marketing function is an educational one. There will be many people in the firm who require this education. The marketing function has many interface areas with other functions (*see* Fig. 13). An example of marketing

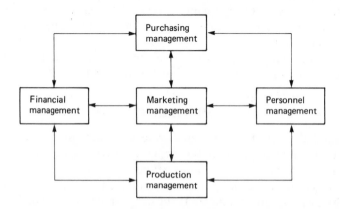

Fig. 13. *Interface between marketing and other functions.*

education for the whole work-force is the Irish Dairy Board, where every employee, including clerical, accounting and personnel staff, is given a marketing course.

In international market penetration, it is also essential to provide thorough product education for agents and customers in overseas markets. In many "turn-key" projects in developing countries, this may mean consultancy and training for five years or more. An example of this was the building and equipping of textile factories in South East Asia by a United Kingdom company. This involved not just supplying the equipment, but installing the complete system, managing the enterprise, and training a technical and managerial counterpart team from the host country.

PENETRATION TACTICS AND THE MARKETING MIX

The maximum potential for each element of the marketing mix is only possible when each is considered in depth. This is particularly important when attempting to penetrate an international market where major adaptation to approaches is often necessary.

Neil H. Borden describes many elements which go to make up the marketing mix, for example product planning, pricing, branding, channels of distribution, selling methods, advertising, promotion, packaging, etc. The choice of this marketing mix is a strategic choice, but its implementation, in the turbulent environment of today, calls for many quick-witted tactical decisions. The time-scale for making these decisions is ever shortening. The electric motor took sixty-five years to progress from invention to commercial exploitation, radar took five years, some computer developments now take three or four months. To borrow a concept from Igor Ansoff in his book *Strategic Management*, a management which is "foresightful" rather than "myopic", will have a better perception of the environment, and so its strategies will be more in tune with that environment.

The closeness of the match between strategy and environment will have an effect on the frequency with which tactical measures must be introduced, and the pressure of the time-scale will effect the quality of those measures, but they must always be introduced in a manner which is compatible with the strategy.

Borden cites some examples of tactical manoeuvres as "a new product, aggressive promotion, reorganisation of sales force, etc.", and says that this type of short-range force plays a large part in fashioning the mix at any time. However, he concludes: "the overall strategy employed in a marketing mix is the product of longer range plans and procedures dictated in part by past empiricism and in part ... by management foresight as to what needs to be done to keep the firm successful in a changing world".

Perhaps the frequency of tactical decisions, and therefore the risk of deviation from strategy, can be lessened if the market strategy and progress towards its fulfilment are carefully monitored. Contingency arrangements should be built into the plan which will minimise or maximise deviations as required. The deviations will be identified by regular monitoring of actual results against forecast company sales and forecast market shares.

The communications mix (*see* Chapter 12 and Fig. 26) is a potential disaster area in countries and languages with their own specific norms and word meanings. In its communication with its customers, and potential customers, a company can make or break itself. Nevertheless, properly designed and implemented communications ideas can be winners. R. Karl Van Leer in "Industrial Marketing with a Flair" (*Harvard Business Review*) describes the "paint scrubber" promotion which enabled a raw-materials manufacturer to achieve considerable market penetration, even though competitors' products were similar in quality and price, by helping customers with *their* marketing problems. Levitt also describes instances of firms offering consultancy services to customer firms. In "Improve Distribution with your Promotional Mix" in the *Harvard Business Review*, Benson P. Shapiro provides a wealth of promotional tactical measures which, properly controlled, could enhance any firm's performance.

APPROACHES TO PENETRATING THE INTERNATIONAL MARKET

Many businesses adopt a cautious approach to the international marketplace, often because of their lack of knowledge and confidence, and to minimise risk of failure and loss. If the approach of minimal involvement and risk is chosen, then the licence for a product can be sold for various world markets. Another approach is to consider a whole range of middlemen, based at home and in the foreign market. The schedule in Fig. 14 gives an overview. The part of the schedule below line (*B*) represents a deeper and more direct involvement. It is often a question of moving from the (*A*) part of the schedule to the (*B*) part, with greater cost and management challenge.

These various mechanisms will be discussed in more detail in Chapter 15.

SUMMARY

This chapter has only briefly discussed a few aspects of the question posed. Auditing of the marketing process has not been discussed, although it is an important tool for ensuring adherence to strategy or, if need be, alteration of strategy. Portfolio analysis, and its effect on tactical decisions could have been discussed, as could market segmentation, product life cycle and many other facets of the marketing process.

However, at least the central theme relating to tactics in market penetration or any other sphere of marketing has been aired; that is that tactical moves must form part of an integrated effort.

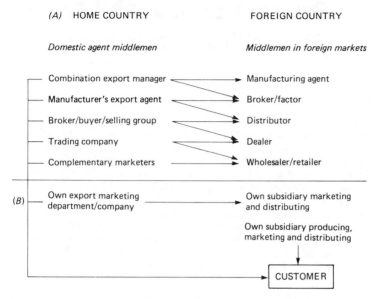

Fig. 14. *Penetrating the international market.*

The last word is given to Theodore Levitt:

No company can afford not to use the more encompassing, consolidating, customer-getting concept of centripetal marketing. And it cannot afford to avoid or constantly postpone developing a clear statement of its goals and directions, otherwise it may wastefully practise centripetal marketing on the wrong products at the wrong time with the wrong results.

Effective and efficient penetration of international markets is central to international marketing.

QUESTIONS

1. You are asked to discuss the German market penetration tactics for a small British manufacturer (sixty employees) of continental quilts.
2. Develop a market penetration plan for the United Kingdom market on behalf of a Thai producer of quality jewellery.

CHAPTER NINE

Production Capability, Flexibility and Pricing

OBJECTIVES

This chapter aims to ensure that the reader understands the importance of systematically assessing production capability, flexibility and pricing as a preliminary to international marketing. There are many examples of medium-sized firms in developing countries being embarrassed by the size of orders, without the production capability to meet them. A proper assessment ensures that if an exporter goes to the market-place, it is with knowledge and confidence about what can be delivered and at what price. The process also helps with the screening and selection of international markets.

Before exporting it is essential to ensure that there is commitment and capability in the top management team—in production as well as marketing management. Without this back-up the international marketer is "out on a limb", and will not have confidence in his production colleagues.

ASSESSING THE R & D CAPABILITY

Research and Development (R & D) is the life blood of the firm. Key questions include the following.

(*a*) Is there time, space, and equipment for assessing new product ideas and adapting present product lines?

(*b*) Are we capable of carrying our present product range?

(*c*) Is there a systematic assessment of where our existing products are in the product life cycle? (*see* Fig. 15)

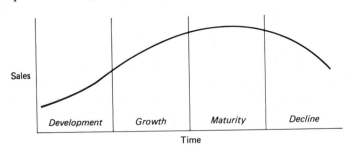

Fig. 15. *The product life cycle.*

(*d*) Have we introduced or phased out any products in the last two years?

(*e*) Is the R & D work relating closely to the market-place and to the production team (*see* Fig. 16)?

(*f*) Have there been any international contacts in the field of R & D in terms of international market trends?

Fig. 16. *R & D relationships.*

It is possible that many smaller firms will not have an R & D section. These questions should then be referred to the production manager or owner.

PRODUCTION SYSTEM—TECHNICAL CAPABILITY

The technical system should be examined to see whether it is up to date in terms of the domestic base or international market context. If it is outmoded and has many breakdowns, there is possibly a case for introducing new technology with greater reliability and quality assurance before going into international markets. In many developing countries, it may essentially be a manual system, incapable of the finer finish demanded by international standards or agencies. An example is the Asian producer of footballs who could not technically meet European standards of finish, even with the best of raw materials (leather).

In addition to quality finish and reliability, the technical capacity for output should also be assessed. Could the output be doubled or trebled, and how does this measure up to a possible international market target? What are the implications for maintenance and skilled staff?

MANAGEMENT AND MANPOWER CAPABILITY

Attitude is one of the key factors in regard to the management/manpower team effort. Has there been full and frank discussion on going international? Is there a keen competitive spirit to succeed against competitors in the international market? Has management been fully involved in the screening and selection of the target market(s)? Has there been an assessment of the skill required, and has there been a management and manpower development plan where this is needed? Where necessary, is it possible to "buy in" the required skill deficits? It should be remembered that the human element is vital to successful international marketing. (*See also* Chapter 17.)

RAW MATERIALS

The systems audit continues with the key area of raw materials, which is often taken for granted in many industrialised countries, but can be critical in some developing countries. This problem of raw material supply in developing countries can be connected with actual access to, or the logistics of, raw material supply, or in many cases with the lack of foreign currency and consequent domestic government import limitations. Even in the industrialised world, sources of supply may be limited, and therefore an over-dependence on one or two sources may mean vulnerability to sudden price changes. A very recent example of this has been the 100 per cent increase in the price of flax from Belgium, and the effect this has had on product development and pricing. It also raises the question of whether or not the United Kingdom could grow its own flax.

Flexibility of raw materials to new product development and adaptation is also an important issue. The quality of raw materials is a further factor to be considered in this respect.

The question of raw materials sourcing and flexibility in supply is important not just at firm level, but also at industrial and national level. Some industries have raw materials research centres paid for by industrial associations. It may be appropriate to consider whether there is enough contact between the firm and these facilities. Similarly, national research centres and policy documents are often developed. In fact, many developing countries have to accompany national export policies with national raw materials sourcing policies. Business leaders should be fully informed of these national priorities.

LABOUR FLEXIBILITY

In planning international marketing activities, it is essential to assess the extent to which there is flexibility in the labour force. This flexibility may be both qualitative and quantitative. As mentioned earlier, there may be a need for more skill for new product and market development, for instance in final finish, presentation and packaging. Is there scope for improving existing skills, or recuiting these new skills in or near the location of the firm? Are there local training centres for skills development, or will the firm have to provide this facility? Are there government grants or other support for skills development? Has the firm got the training capacity in trainers, and facilities to accomplish the task?

Likewise, quantitatively, the question might be put, can the firm double turnover at short notice, e.g. by introducing a two- or three-shift system and taking on more workers? How skilled are these new workers likely to be? How quickly can the new work-force be made effective? How will this expansion affect wages?

The whole question of labour flexibility is in a sense related to the state of the firm's technology. A more up-to-date "generation" of technology has been known to be capable of doubling output with half the work-force. The man/machine ratio can change overnight. With this flexibility and the recession of the late 1970s and 1980s, it might be stated that labour market pricing is more flexible now than for many a decade. However, it varies between industries and countries. Many would argue that labour flexibility was always a feature of exporting organisations in developing countries.

PRICING FOR INCREASED OUTPUT

This topic is dealt with in detail in Chapter 16. However, it is useful here to emphasise that the whole area of production capability analysis and flexibility for expanded output can have a drastic impact on overall pricing strategy.

One of the most favourable contexts is the domestic firm which is producing for a limited home market and operating at 50 per cent or less capacity. In this instance, with no further scope in the domestic market, it simply does not make sense *not* to go into international markets, as resources are not being fully utilised (*see* Fig. 17). The temptation is then to

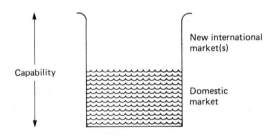

Fig. 17. *Domestic market below capability.*

charge only the marginal cost and a percentage for export market penetration, as the overheads are already absorbed by domestic sales. Although this is consistent with a short-term strong market share competitive position in the international market (as is evident in some Japanese business policies), it is dangerous to ignore the longer-term consequences when present capacity is inadequate and a complete overhaul and expansion of production is needed with new overheads.

The challenge is to plan for some phasing and consistency between short-term competitiveness/penetration and longer-term profitability across all markets—domestic and international.

SUMMARY

This chapter has concentrated on a systematic and questioning approach to various key factors of production capability, which is often inadequately carried out by existing and potential exporters. All key factors are interactive on one another (*see* Fig. 18).

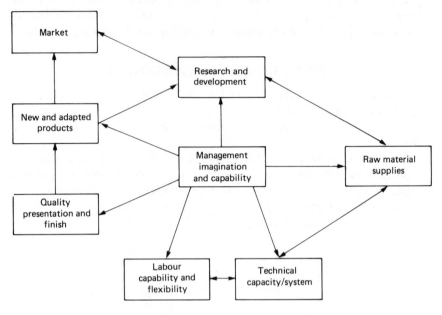

Fig. 18. *Key factors of production capability.*

Financial aspects were considered briefly in regard to pricing. However, these will be examined more fully in Chapters 13 and 16.

QUESTIONS

1. Discuss your systematic production capability appraisal as a potential United Kingdom exporter of gents' shirts for the German market.

2. Advise an aspiring Sri Lankan exporter of footballs to the United Kingdom market on his capability appraisal.

CHAPTER TEN

International
Market Research

OBJECTIVES

This chapter aims to explain the process of international market research in the context of the total international marketing system. While outlining a possible planning framework, the complexities of researching international markets will be apparent compared to domestic market research. It is important that all aspects of the framework are flexible and by no means prescriptive, as the challenges of international market research vary between countries, industries and projects.

INTERNATIONAL MARKET RESEARCH IN CONTEXT

To develop a plan of action for international market research without putting it into context is akin to going to see merely the middle act of a three-act play. The exercise only has meaning if Act 1 (the company's motives, home market track record and commitment to international marketing) is known, while Act 3 will set the scene for the current developments in international marketing or global marketing that any firm may have to face at home or abroad.

There would appear to be a consensus in international marketing that "No useful purpose is to be served by segregating exporting from the mainstream of marketing practice, and that marketing in foreign environments should be approached in exactly the same way as marketing at home" (M. J. Baker, *Marketing: An Introductory Text*). Similarly, "Marketing is a process of twofold character, technical and social; marketing technology, the application of principles, rules or knowledge relating to the non-human elements of marketing, has universal validity and potentially universal applicability" (Baker, *Journal of Marketing*, July 1968).

If there are universal principles for marketing, whether in the home or foreign market, then the first question for any firm must be: "Is the home market practice sufficiently sound to form the basis for an international venture?"

There is considerable evidence to suggest that in the United Kingdom the emphasis on marketing, and in particular market research, leaves a great deal to be desired. The British Institute of Management report *Marketing Organisation in British Industry* (1970) states:

> In view of the frequent references to the increasingly competitive nature of the business environment, one might expect that the majority of firms would have a marketing research department—in fact remarkably few do. In the survey of 265

major companies, 74 per cent undertook market research, but only 38 per cent had appointed somebody full-time to this activity.

Perhaps the answer is that the research is commissioned from specialist firms. However, in 1977 this amounted to a mere £55 million in Britain.

In most firms, the home market is usually the main market, and if the market research plan in this sphere has not been well developed, what hope is there for the international field? The textbook theory on international market research should be kept in perspective with known home practice. J. M. Livingstone lends weight to such caution:

> Often the decision to try a market arises from a discussion of the question with a business acquaintance who has experience of a particular market, and on no greater research than a recommendation of this sort, the newcomer will decide to try the same market. The "me too" effect in deciding to export and in choosing a market should not be underestimated.

The international research plan should have as a framework a clearly defined idea of the identity of the firm and the way it operates in the home market, and an understanding of the capabilities and resources it can employ if a suitable market is identified. Obviously there will be as many frameworks as there are firms, and the decision to enter the international market may arise from any combination of a number of factors. M. J. Baker outlines the following reasons why firms have, historically, looked towards international markets.

(a) Loss of domestic market share because of increased competition.

(b) Loss of domestic market share because of product obsolescence or product life cycle.

(c) Saturisation of domestic markets precluding the attainment of scale economies.

(d) The provision of incentives, e.g. grant subsidy for exporters ("push") or tax relief by host groups ("pull").

(e) Potential demand linked by purchasing power, usually in three forms:
　　(i) need for equivalent product at a lower price;
　　(ii) better product at a competitive price;
　　(iii) product not available in the foreign market.

Having decided to go into international markets, there are two levels of international market research necessary: the *macro level* of broad screening and selection of markets, and the *micro level* of investigating each individual market selected. These stages may be seen in Fig. 19, which outlines the whole context.

There follows a brief discussion on the screening of markets, but the major part of the rest of the chapter examines the planning framework for market research in a selected international market.

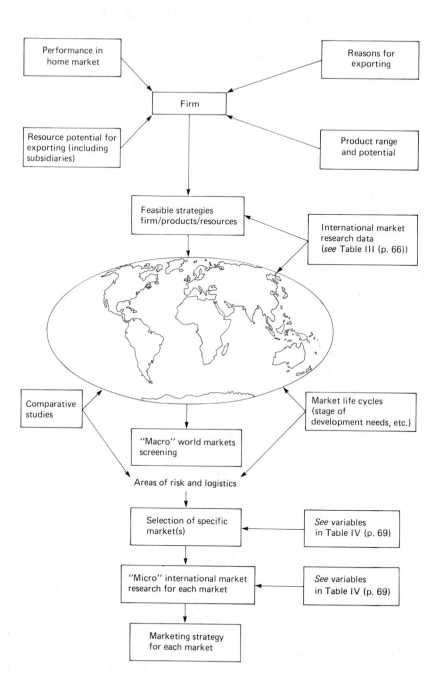

Fig. 19. *International market research.*

INVESTIGATING THE MOST PROMISING MARKETS

Table III gives some idea of the vast range of data sources for the investigation of the most promising markets.

TABLE III. COMMONLY USED DATA SOURCES FOR
INTERNATIONAL MARKET RESEARCH

Guide to Official Statistics
Monthly Digest of Statistics
Overseas Trade Statistics
Social Trends
Statistical News
Trade and Industry
United Kingdom Balance of Payments
Balance of Payments Yearbook (IMF)
EEC and ECSC publications
International Financial Statistics (IMF)
International Labour Review
International Travel Statistics
United Nations Yearbook of National Accounts Statistics
United Nations Yearbook of International Trade Statistics
United Nations Demographic Yearbook
United Nations Directory of International Trade
United Nations National Statistic Yearbook
United Nations Statistical Papers
Yearbook of International Trade Statistics
Yearbook of Fisheries
Yearbook of Forest Product Statistics
Yearbook of Food and Agricultural Statistics
Yearbook of Labour Statistics
Abstract of Regional Statistics (1975)
Annual Abstract of Statistics
Blue Book on National Income and Expenditure
British Labour Statistics Yearbook
Business Monitor
Censuses of Distribution, Population and Production
Department of Employment Gazette
Economic Trends
Financial Statistics
International organisations and overseas agencies' publications

With the knowledge of why the firm wants to enter the international marketing field, and the resources or backing that they may be able to muster for the "how" of the operation, it is now possible to start to look at the "where" aspect of the operation. The most obvious starting-point for any United Kingdom firm will be the British Overseas Trade Board (BOTB), which offers numerous services, including a free overseas Marketing Research Advisory Service, financial support for export marketing research and management support services (*see also* Chapter 19).

Obviously the reasons why a firm wishes to export its product(s) and the resources it can accumulate for the exercise may be critical factors in deciding the breadth of the research. For the moment, however, let us assume that the firm in question is neither a global giant, capable of exploiting need by creating totally new products, nor a short-term "dumper of excess production" until the home market settles, but an average firm somewhere in the middle, with the motivation to grow and with the resources that such a firm might be expected to muster.

The options open to such a firm for narrowing the field of international market investigation may be one or a combination of the following:

(a) market life cycle identification;
(b) comparative analysis;
(c) investigation of the most promising markets.

The market life cycle identification framework is based on the concept of the product life cycle, and the clustering of world markets. The concept and framework can also be used for locating markets such as those provided by both developing and industrialised countries. This analysis tool (in the context of the firm's motivation, resources and back-up) helps identify those areas in the world where demand may be at the development, growth, maturity or decline stage for the firm's product(s).

S. Majaro and R. D. Buzzell follow a matrix screening method to identify target markets. Starting on a global basis, they use a comparison system to identify differences in markets which may be critical in the marketing of products (see Fig. 20).

Majaro goes further and develops a comparative analysis system, using a bench-mark norm, either based on the home, or an existing market, or on markets where the product or approach has been adapted. Using this system, it should be possible to identify areas where products *may* have a possible chance. At this point, it must be stressed that getting to this stage may be more difficult than suggested. Comparative analysis is only possible if detailed information is available.

Holloway and Hancock state:

> The range of the quality of marketing research is staggering, from almost nothing to the most sophisticated practices. Eastern European nations including the USSR have increased their marketing research efforts in the last decade: research in Far Eastern countries is erratic and arbitrary, but improving both in quality and quantity. Research in Great Britain and Western European nations is *quite* good.

In reviewing the "do's" and "dont's" of international marketing, many consultants recommend that firms should not be too ambitious, and that marketing efforts should be centred on no more than *three* ventures to ensure that there is sufficient impact and to minimise the risks of spreading resources too thinly. In addition, the cautious firm would be well advised to reflect on the BIM definition of market research for a specific market: "The objective gathering, recording and analysing of all facts about problems

Factors limiting standardisation	Product design	Pricing	Distribution	Sales force	Advertising and promotion, branding and packaging
Market characteristics					
Physical environment	Climate; Product use conditions		Customer mobility	Dispersion of customers	Access to media; Climate
Stage of economic and industrial development	Income levels; labour costs in relation to capital costs	Income levels	Consumer shopping patterns	Wage levels; availability of manpower	Needs for convenience rather than economy; purchasing quantities
Cultural factors	Custom and tradition; attitudes towards foreign goods	Attitudes towards bargaining	Consumer shopping patterns	Attitudes towards selling	Language, literacy symbolism
Industry conditions					
Stage of product life cycle in each market	Extent of product differentiation	Elasticity of demand	Availability of outlets	Need for missionary sales effort	Awareness, experience with products
Competition	Quality levels	Local costs; price of substitutes	Desirability of private brands; Competitors' control of outlets	Competitors sales force	Competitive expenditures; messages
Marketing institutions					
Distributive system	Availability of outlets	Prevailing margins	Number and variety of outlets available; Ability to "force" distribution	Number, size, dispersion of outlets	Extent of self-service
Advertising, media and agencies				Effectiveness of advertising, need for substitutes	Media availability, costs; overlaps
Legal restriction	Product standards, patent laws, tariffs and taxes	Tariffs and anti-trust laws; resale price maintenance	Restrictions on product lines; resale price maintenance	General employment restrictions; specific restrictions on selling	Specific restrictions on messages, costs; trademark laws

Source: Harvard Business Review, Vol. 46, Nov.–Dec. 1968, pp. 108–109.

Fig. 20. *Factors limiting standardisation in international marketing.*

relating to the transfer and sale of goods (consumer and industrial) and services from producer to consumer or user."

TABLE IV: VARIABLES TO CONSIDER IN INTERNATIONAL MARKETS

Financial considerations
Capital acquisition plan
Length of payback period
Projected cash inflows (years one, two, etc.)
Projected cash outflows (years one, two, etc.)
Return of investment
Monetary exchange considerations

Technical and engineering feasibility considerations
Raw materials availability (construction/support/supplies)
Raw materials availability (products)
Geography/climate
Site locations and access
Availability of local labour
Availability of local management
Economic infrastructure (roads, water, electricity, etc.)
Facilities planning (preliminary or detailed)

Marketing considerations
Market size
Market potential
Distribution costs
Competition
Time necessary to estimate sales channels
Promotion costs
Social/cultural factors impacting upon products

Economic and legal considerations
Legal systems
Host government attitudes towards foreign investment
Host attitude toward this particular investment
Restrictions on ownership
Tax laws
Import/export restrictions
Capital flow restrictions
Land-title acquisitions
Inflation

Political and social considerations
International political stability
Relations with neighbouring countries
Political, social traditions
Communist influence
Religious/racial/language homogeneity
Labour organisations and attitudes
Skill/technical level of labour force
Socio-economic infrastructure to support American families

Source: James R. Piper Jnr. "How US firms evaluate foreign market opportunities." *MSU Business Topics*, Vol. 19 (Summer 1971), p. 14.

James R. Piper outlines a detailed checklist which firms should consider in analysing foreign market opportunities and limitations (*see* Table IV). However, as M. J. Baker acknowledges, "as most market research is concerned with the specific investigation of all factors which infringe upon the marketing of goods, the scale of the function is limitless." Most firms with limited resources will be satisfied if they can get a rough perception of the profitability of the market and identify the key problem areas which may require careful attention.

Today, most governments recognise the benefits of having a healthy balance of payments, and consequently the industrial firm will find that there are numerous government and other agencies that can be of help in compiling and assessing the market of a particular country. Through these sources the cautious firm should be able to make a comprehensive assessment of the risks and suitability of a specific market. However, J. M. Livingstone cautions against the collection of superfluous information, even if it is available, and advocates that the firm carefully considers "what market research is really necessary and what precisely it is being used to establish". He suggests further that in practice the following are the key areas of research which should be explored, depending on the product.

(*a*) The size and nature of the market in terms of age, sex, income, occupation and social status of consumers.

(*b*) The geographical location of potential consumers.

(*c*) The market shares of major competitors (local and international), and prices.

(*d*) The structure, capacity and organisation of distributive channels servicing the market.

(*e*) The nature of legal, economic, environmental and cultural trends affecting the structure of the market.

PLANNING FRAMEWORK FOR RESEARCH IN A SELECTED OVERSEAS MARKET

The framework outlined below might assist with the development of a systematic plan for an international market research project. It is essential to hold sight of the specific objective throughout the analysis of national and international data. In some cases, the quality of desk research might be so good that very little, if any, field research is necessary, given the budget and cost benefit analysis. Care should be taken with field research to ensure that, where possible, local teams are recruited to allow for accuracy in recording cultural values and language/communications problems.

INTERNATIONAL MARKET RESEARCH PROJECT PLAN

1. Specific definition of objective. ⎫ *What* information is needed?
                                     ⎪ *Where* can this be found?
2. An outline of the range of sub- ⎨ *How* can it be obtained?
   jects to be covered.   ⎭ *When* can and should it be obtained?

3. *Timetable for principal stages.*
   (*a*) Desk research
   - (*i*) Published data
   - (*ii*) Unpublished data
   - (*iii*) Considering data gaps
   - (*iv*) Competitor infrastructure
   - (*v*) Sample frame

   (*b*) Field research
   - (*i*) Field programme plans
   - (*ii*) Quality/quantity
   - (*iii*) Logistics

   (*c*) Collection, analysis and drafting the report
   - (*i*) Computer technology
   - (*ii*) Presentation plan

   (*d*) Initial presentation meeting
   - Diagnosis of criticisms

   (*e*) Revising and finalising the report
   - (*i*) Graphics and visuals
   - (*ii*) Final printing

   (*f*) Presentation to board (users)
   - (*i*) Main findings
   - (*ii*) Follow-up

ESTIMATING MARKET POTENTIAL

Some basic questions need to be answered which cut through all the macro statistics, and get down to individual buyer behaviour, with regard to an export market.

(*a*) Will people buy the product?

(*b*) How should we change the product to make people more likely to buy it?

(*c*) Why should they buy this product rather than a competitive one?

(*d*) How much will they buy, and how often at particular times in the future?

(*e*) How much will they be prepared to pay for the product?

(*f*) How much money can we expect to earn from those sales?

(*g*) What will be the best ways to market the product, and what marketing costs will be involved?

(*h*) What investment decisions may be required if the product must be modified in order to make it suitable for the market?

A wide range of factors can affect a product's prospect in the market, or the suitability of various marketing options. Factors which may limit market potential for an exporter can be grouped together, as shown in Fig. 21. Each of these factors and their sub-elements are worthy of investigation. However, some may be more important than others, depending on the circumstances of the project—industry, country, industrial or consumer product or service, whether in a developing country or an industrialised nation.

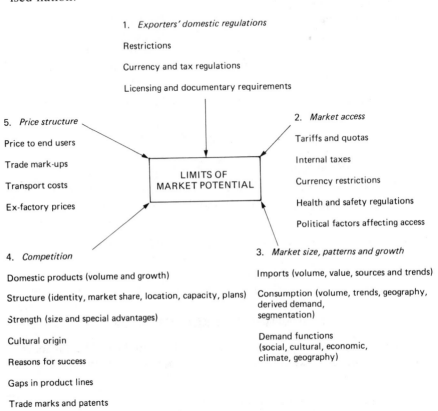

Fig. 21. *Factors limiting market potential.*

PRODUCT RESEARCH

Many product preferences have their roots in traditional, subliminal or environmental factors. This is all the more complex in the many varied cultures which constitute the wide range of world markets. Most product preferences can be grouped as shown in Fig. 22.

In many cultures, colours have specific meanings. There are wide and distinct variations in taste preferences in various parts of the globe. Variations in size often reflect large variations in human measurements. A consignment of ladies' brassières had to be returned by Poland to its Asian exporter, as they were far too tight for the larger Polish busts. Design and style vary considerably in garments and other consumer goods. Government and consumer concern over health and hygiene can affect materials

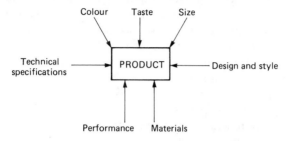

Fig. 22. *Product preferences.*

selection. Cotton shirts are preferred to synthetic fibre in some European countries. Performance and technical considerations vary according to legal and other specifications of various countries. These will be discussed further in the next chapter, together with aspects of packaging and packing.

INVESTIGATION OF MARKETING PRACTICES

It is essential to follow the targeting and product adaptation process with an investigation of marketing practices. These are discussed in detail in later chapters. However, a summary is useful here to complete the framework of the plan for international market research. The following is an outline of such marketing practices.

(*a*) *Transport.*
   (*i*) Freight rates.
   (*ii*) Speed and frequency.
   (*iii*) Reliability.
   (*iv*) Risks.
   (*v*) Packing requirements.
(*b*) *Sales and distribution channels.*
   (*i*) Normal channels for the product (for each element: function, share of sales, changes in importance).
   (*ii*) Alternative channels.
   (*iii*) Advantages, disadvantages and feasibility of using normal or alternative channels.
   (*iv*) Support functions performed by each element in the distribution channel (technical services, advertising and promotion, financial).
   (*v*) Stock levels held by each element.

   (*vi*) Delivery time requirements.
  (*vii*) Mark-ups and discounts at each level.
 (*viii*) Credit facilities and terms of sale expected.
   (*ix*) Major distributors (profiles of the most important ones and
         those most suitable to handle your product: size of the firm,
         sales growth, product line, sales force, type of customers,
         geographic coverage, service facilities, position in the market,
         regulations, possible conflicts of interest, etc.).
(*c*) *Pricing strategy factors.*
    (*i*) Practical limits.
   (*ii*) Supply of competing products.
  (*iii*) Prices of competing products.
   (*iv*) Likely reactions of competitors.
    (*v*) Product advantages.
(*d*) *Advertising and sales promotion.*
    (*i*) Amount of money being spent to support competing products
         (including expenditure as a percentage of company sales).
   (*ii*) Media and techniques mainly used, and the breakdown of ex-
         penditure among them.
  (*iii*) Timing and geographic concentration.
   (*iv*) Sales messages emphasised in advertising of important
         competitors.
    (*v*) Breakdown of expenditure between suppliers, distributors and
         retailers.
(*e*) *Services expected by buyers.*
    (*i*) Technical advice.
   (*ii*) Replacement of defective merchandise.
  (*iii*) Guarantees.
   (*iv*) Repair, maintenance and spare parts.
    (*v*) Training of operators.

DESK AND FIELD RESEARCH

Desk and field research plans impact upon each other. As mentioned earlier, the quality of desk research data might well mean minimum field research work. However, it is useful here to examine briefly both areas.

In the case of desk research, there is a proliferation of data and reports, and discernment is the challenge from both published and unpublished works. The key to success in this area is knowing how to find the sources and how to exploit them fully. Sources include the company's own records and files, and institutional sources, including those listed earlier. The more experienced exporting company has very effective internal records and maintains a continuously updated desk research provision. Export development agencies in various countries supply invaluable desk research back-up.

Field research can often go much deeper than desk research, but of course it is much more expensive, as it involves collecting information, primarily through contact with people. In a distant market, this can be particularly costly. It may be undertaken by the exporting company, or by some agency on behalf of the company. In either case, it should be preceded by desk research at home and in the target market. It might be said that "good market research, like charity, begins at home".

In planning overseas field research, the key networks and gaps in existing desk research must be identified. In addition to the usual questionnaire design, interview planning, logistics of transport and accommodation, a thorough briefing in cultural background and language is important. Alternatively, it may be more effective to use local specialists for the usual range of techniques—personal and telephone interviews, postal surveys, store checks and other direct forms of observation.

USING RESEARCH AGENCIES

There are many reasons why a research agency might be chosen, including:

(*a*) expertise in local customs and trading contacts;
(*b*) language;
(*c*) cost-effectiveness;
(*d*) objectivity.

Selection procedures are important, using all possible sources of information. Initial interviews with a pre-selected listing should be followed by written proposals covering:

(*a*) terms of reference and methodology;
(*b*) time and budget to complete the project;
(*c*) staffing;
(*d*) internal and final report deadlines.

Regular monitoring is advisable.

A detailed research checklist for selecting a market research agency has been prepared by P. A. Management Consultants International (London), which includes, among many other factors:

(*a*) reputation for integrity;
(*b*) indications of ability;
(*c*) experience of organisation;
(*d*) professional aggressiveness;
(*e*) adaptability for project considered;
(*f*) adequacy and convenience of facilities;
(*g*) financial strength;
(*h*) business methods.

Although using market research agencies may be expensive, the overall advantages often outweigh the costs.

SUMMARY

It is important to note that both the initial screening of possible international markets and the more detailed research methods applied to the one, two or three selected markets are the keys to the formation and implementation of plans in this crucial area of international marketing. In both contexts the skill involved is best learned by doing, and preferably as part of a group where the complexities of the operation can be discussed. Some business owners are pleased to have a team of students who will assist them in this process, while obtaining guidance from their local college. It is a process of reciprocal benefit.

QUESTIONS

1. Advise a local micro software company on the development of an initial export market screening process.
2. Plan the possible follow-up export market research for two selected markets.

CHAPTER ELEVEN

Product Development, Adaptation, Design and Packaging

OBJECTIVES

This chapter aims to help the reader understand the various facets of product development, adaptation and design for an export market, together with the packaging and packing considerations so vital for exporting. The topics discussed follow on naturally from the previous chapter on international market research, as any new product or adapted product should relate to market need. The feasibility of product adaptation and new product development is examined in relation to the capability of the firm. The area of product design presentation and packaging is also related to market preference. Product testing, financial control and the possibility of contract manufacturing are all vital considerations in export product development.

PRODUCT POLICY AND MARKET NEEDS

Most firms will find it easier and less risky to develop variations on existing products than to establish completely new product types. With the former, markets already exist and the exporter who can offer significant advantages over current ones should prosper. For example, Japanese cars have been quite successful in recent years, as many are convinced they are better value for money. It would have been much harder for the Japanese to produce a completely new kind of land transportation.

The components of a product are many from the buyer's point of view—the physical care, packaging, after-sales service, brand name, image of product in the buyer's mind, and the benefits he/she thinks it will give.

As mentioned earlier, products often have a life cycle in a particular market (*see* Chapter 9, Fig. 15). When a product is at the decline stage, the firm may need to withdraw it, organise a drastic adaptation for a new demand/segment, or adapt it for another market where it might enter at the growth stage with some likelihood of success.

There are three basic categories of objectives in product development (*see also* Fig. 23).:

(*a*) policy objectives, which provide a broad framework and long-term goals;

(*b*) operational objectives in terms of immediate impact on the company's operations (includes market-oriented objectives, discussed in more detail below);

(*c*) impact objectives which define the effect a new product should have on the market.

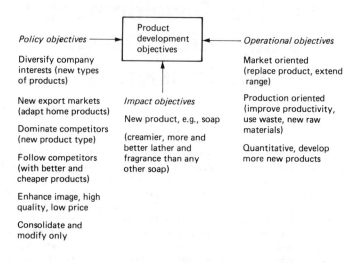

Fig. 23. *Categories of product development objective.*

MARKET-ORIENTED OBJECTIVES

Product development projects should usually aim at achieving marketing-oriented objectives. The most common of these are to:

(*a*) replace a failed product;
(*b*) revitalise a successful product;
(*c*) adapt a product for a new market or a new market segment;
(*d*) extend or complete a range of products;
(*e*) create a new range of products distinct from but compatible with the existing range;
(*f*) enter a new business;
(*g*) meet or beat competition.

OBTAINING NEW PRODUCT IDEAS

A regular flow of new ideas is important. Some sources of new ideas include the following.

(*a*) A company's market research office which should have an overall view of markets and trends.

(*b*) In-company suggestion schemes arising from the workers' clear perspective of products and their potential for modification.

(*c*) The company's sales force and agents who are often up to date on customers' unsatisfied needs.

(*d*) A company's technical development department, dealing with technical advances and improvements in existing products.

(*e*) Customers' reaction to product range (for example, the "man-size Kleenex" came from a complaint that the product was too small).

(*f*) Competition—range of products and customers' reaction (small companies often follow large firms' innovation and learn from mistakes of others).

(*g*) Research and educational institutions, including centres such as science parks (many examples exist from plastics and rubber technology research).

Many small firms can benefit from these sources. It is the receptive and searching nature of the business leaders which counts, not the scale of operation. However, the business should also structure itself to reorganise and utilise new ideas. Figure 24 shows how this can be done.

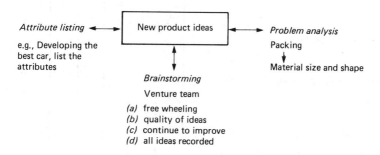

Fig. 24. *Obtaining new product ideas.*

SCREENING NEW PRODUCT IDEAS

In screening, the firm should seek to minimise two types of error: drop errors and go errors. The drop error is dismissing an otherwise good idea because of lack of vision. An example was the turning down by Decca of the Beatles in 1962. A go error is when a poor idea is allowed to proceed through the design stage.

There are two stages in the screening process:

(*a*) relating the product idea to the firm's objectives, finances and capability; and

(*b*) relating the idea to the firm's competitive strong points.

In *stage one* the following questions should be considered.

(*a*) Is there compatibility with the firm's objectives in terms of:
    (*i*) profitability (return on investment);
    (*ii*) volume and stability of sales;
    (*iii*) sales growth;
    (*iv*) effect on existing product range;
    (*v*) effect on corporate image?

(*b*) How compatible is the idea with available financial resources for commercialisation?

(*c*) How compatible is the idea with available technical and professional staff for commercialisation?

Stage two is concerned with the consistency of the idea with the competitive strong points of the firm. The firm's strengths and weaknesses are included in a screening matrix (*see* example in Fig. 25). The venture team (*see* Fig. 24) should be from various specialist areas, to give a broad and objective view of weightings and compatibility values.

Sphere of performance (A)	Weighting	Very good 10	Good 8	Fair 6	Poor 4	Very poor 2	Rating (A x B)
Company personality	(2)			✓			12
Marketing	(2)	✓					20
Research and development	(2)		✓				16
Personnel	1.0			✓			6
Finance	1.5	✓					15
Production	0.5		✓				4
Location and facilities	0.5				✓		2
Purchasing and supply	0.5	✓					5
							80

Rating scale: 0-40 poor;　41-75 fair;

76-100 good,　proceed to design.

Fig. 25. *Screening matrix.*

PRODUCT ADAPTATION AND DESIGN

As has already been mentioned, such adaptations may be much more feasible than devising completely new product types. Adaptations should be based on market preferences identified through market research. Product adaptation will obviously be more economic in markets where preferences are close to the domestic market norms, changes may then be minimal. Another possibility is to choose a cluster of two or three markets with similar preferences. In this way similar adaptations are possible for more than one market, which might help with longer runs of standard adaptations. As indicated earlier, product adaptations can include one or more combinations of the following: colour, size, taste, design and style, materials, performance and technological specification.

Many developing countries have trouble in achieving the correct adaptation and presentation for the industrialised markets. Similarly, European exporters to South East Asia need to adapt drastically some industrial products—to intermediate technology level for least developed countries. An example of adaptation for the Third World is the Tinkabi tractor (*see* Appendix III).

Product adaptation to meet new market or segment needs is an exciting part of product development.

PACKAGING AND PACKING CONSIDERATIONS

Other aspects of product research include *packaging*, meaning the final product pack (presentation), and *packing* for shipment. The product design should be based on the customer's needs. In industrial products, the pack should be considered for its usage, and for its amenability to storing, pouring, re-use, etc. For consumer products, the pack might have various functions: protective, informative, merchandising and conforming to legal requirements and buying habits (for example, Americans tend to buy less frequently than Europeans, so the largest size is more popular in the United States).

Quality packing for shipment is vital, even in this day of containerisation and air freight systems. Poor quality packing can mean poor quality product, costly delivery and storage, and failure to meet legal requirements. There are many examples of goods such as soaps and vegetable oils which were poorly packed by Third World countries, and ended as waste in the holds of ships.

"Invisible" products or services such as tourism, banking, insurance, processing zones and so on can be similarly appraised in the above overall framework when trying to estimate market potential.

PRODUCT TESTING

Product testing is concerned with the following basic questions.

(*a*) Does the product (and/or its packaging) have the qualities and performance intended by the producer?

(*b*) Will it satisfy the target buyers?

(*c*) In what respect should it be changed if the above answers are negative?

Testing should be undertaken regularly during a product's development. Testing physical and technical qualities is vital, often from a legal point of view. Subjecting it to the real-life situation, as well as laboratory testing, is important. Industrial customers and consumers alike are often keen to participate in the testing process.

Specialist agencies for prototype testing are a very worthwhile investment for some projects, often with the help of an importer or agent. Such tests may include trade fairs, public place/town hall tests, shop tests and surveys, retailer reactions, and factory tests. It is important that tests cover the packaging process, and also transhipment packing for product production.

FINANCIAL CONTROL

The whole cycle of product development, adaptation and testing can be very expensive. It is important to keep an eye on the cost of the investment and probable rate of return. Whatever the source of finance, the firm must be in a position to judge a programme against the cost of financing it. Discounted cash flow is based on the simple principle that £100 in a year's time is not as valuable at £100 today. It is possible thus to relate future revenue in today's value to present development costs. Further details of export financing are included in Chapter 13.

SUMMARY

The reader will have noted the key relationship between market needs, product policy and product development. The systematic approach to obtaining and screening new product ideas is a challenging and costly area. The lower risk policy of product adaptation is vital for regular review of the product portfolio; incorporated in this adaptation are the packaging and packing aspects. Finally, product testing and financial control are essential factors of product development in these years of ever-increasing costs.

QUESTIONS

1. As a manager of a children's toy factory, discuss how you might approach the product development area in terms of a European export market (EEC member state).

2. You are asked as a future textile machinery factory manager to analyse product adaptation possibilities for a country in a nascent stage of development.

CHAPTER TWELVE

The Marketing Communication Mix

OBJECTIVES

Having researched the export market and adapted/developed the appropriate product in terms of design and packaging, it is now important to plan and organise how to communicate with the market-place. This chapter examines the range of marketing communication mechanisms, and discusses selection and adaptation of the optimum mix for maximum impact in a potential export market. The financial implications will be examined in Chapters 13 and 16.

ELEMENTS OF THE
MARKETING COMMUNICATION MIX

Promotion/communications is a key subset of the marketing mix (*see* Chapter 8) and includes the elements outlined in Fig. 26. These seven elements each have their respective strengths and weaknesses.

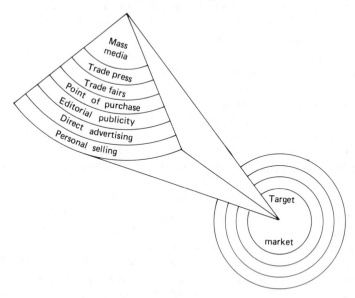

Fig. 26. *Promotions mix.*

Personal selling is the most direct, and often the most effective, means of communication. However, it is only possible to reach a limited number of people and this is therefore an inefficient way to create a demand to pull sales through the distribution channels. Nevertheless, this method may be appropriate for specialist products or services where there are a few key influential buyers. An example would be large government contracts. All other mechanisms are of an indirect nature, working through third parties, where the challenge is to create enthusiasm and commitment.

Direct advertising is used where the marketing communication can be aimed at named customers. Good examples include sales literature, direct mail, and samples and gifts. Sales literature is usually well-presented printed material, catalogues and leaflets in the language and style of the target market. This is often used with certain income groups chosen from, for example, American Express lists. It may be distributed by direct mail, personal calls or exhibitions. Direct mail means using the postal service with specific mailing lists for the target market. Samples and gifts are a valuable form of advertising, and are often sent through the post, or given at trade fairs or in-store promotions. The more unusual or useful the gift, the more effective the promotion.

Editorial publicity can be a most effective form of communication, using public relations to gain editorial space. Editorial publicity is news of a topical nature about the exporter's company, product or service which might be featured on television or radio or in the trade press. This process is often the result of good press relations and a well-prepared, imaginative press release. It is a relatively inexpensive method of marketing communications, but has to be well planned through press receptions and direct contact with news media editors.

Point-of-purchase promotions include special events and demonstrations in retail stores, supported by good display stands and materials. It is most effective because the customer is, it is hoped, being influenced at his purchasing decision point. This method is often part of a co-ordinated effort, in harness with media advertising and special retail offers. A good example in 1984 was where a United Kingdom county had a special export week in a large department store in a twinned area in West Germany. The event included cultural displays, music and dancing, and craft goods demonstrations.

Trade fairs and exhibitions in overseas markets are a fruitful way of showing the effectiveness of products and services. Many are internationally famous, e.g. Hanover and Leipzig in Europe, and specialist fairs such as the Cologne Food Fair, the Paris Textile Fair and the Frankfurt Book Fair. Fairs serve disparate purposes—sales promotion, market penetration, establishing contact with agents, selling and product testing. They are also useful for getting to know what the competition is offering, and—in planned economies—making the acquaintance of the state-buying organisations and their business leaders.

The trade press can be one of the most important media, with reasonable rates and specialised readership; thus the exporter is *target* marketing. The trade press includes trade magazines, newspapers and newsletters for particular interest groups, trades, professions and industries.

The mass media is the opposite to the highly selective trade press in that, as the name suggests, its target is large numbers of the public with usually expensive rates of advertising. There are, however, possible uses for the mass media, even when definite market segments have been identified. This is feasible when a particular type of mass media is read by a segment of the population, e.g. the *Financial Times* for business leaders, a specialist page in a particular newspaper, or a particular time of day on a particular television channel.

Media selection is a highly skilled area often best left, in the case of mass media, to advertising agents.

Sponsorship is emerging as a growing area of promotions. It is particularly useful in promoting goods which cannot be freely advertised because of legal restrictions. Examples are:

(*a*) Canon Football League;
(*b*) Brittanic Assurance County Cricket Championship;
(*c*) Embassy World Snooker Championship;
(*d*) Carrolls Irish Open Golf Championship;
(*e*) Jameson Open Snooker Championship;
(*f*) Suntory World Matchplay Golf Championship.

However, when sponsorship is too intensive in sport, it can give an over-commercialised image. This was one reaction to the 1984 Olympics, where there were a wide range of sponsors, including McDonald's (food), Fuji (films), Anheuser-Busch (beer), Coca-Cola (soft drinks) and Colt (cars). Nevertheless, sponsorship of sport and sporting events continues to be an effective and popular promotions tool in many parts of the world.

SELECTING THE OPTIMUM MIX

The starting-point in selecting the optimum communication mix must again be the target market and audience. The international marketer will have a range to consider from examples such as:

(*a*) agents who are in a similar business and who may be interested in handling the product or service;
(*b*) industrial buyers who use the same or similar products;
(*c*) wholesalers or retailers from the same industry, whom an exporter would wish to encourage to stock the particular product; and
(*d*) particular groups of consumers in a selected distribution area, or from certain income groups, whose needs require satisfaction by the product or service.

Depending on the selected distribution policy, and to what extent middlemen are involved, rather than the final customer, separate marketing communications may need to be designed to achieve the "push" effect by middlemen, and the "pull" effect by consumers. It is possible that both may be needed, using a combination of the above methods.

The choice of methods may well need to be a compromise which satisfies the following requirements:

(a) reaching the target market most precisely;
(b) using the most effective method of communications in physical terms; and
(c) staying within the prescribed budget.

In addition, there may have to be a compromise between *breadth* (contacting the total target audience) and *depth* (contacting a smaller, but influential group, specifically selected).

An example of the "push" through middlemen and "pull" by potential customers is the export marketing of cars, e.g. Rover cars in the United States market. It might be argued that the De Lorean car enjoyed a fair share of "push" through the middlemen (agents) in the United States, but not enough "pull" through the channels by the potential customers.

Much of the marketing mix is irrelevant when a firm seeks to tender for Third World projects financed through the EEC, the United Nations or the World Bank. What is important then is the direct approach in tender documents, and well-presented, colourful specifications, fitting the requirements of both the financing agency and the Third World government department. Quality after-sales service and contract management could be critical aspects of the image to be projected.

ADAPTATION TO THE MARKET SETTING

In *International Marketing—A Comparative Systems Approach*, David Carson comments that:

> The socioeconomic shortcomings of advertising and sales promotion are most obvious in their excesses in Western nations, especially in the United States where they hold uniquely strong positions. On the contrary, it is in the nations where advertising and sales promotion are unusually weak that their socioeconomic values are most readily apparent.

In developing countries such as India there is little demand creation. The philosophy of life is less materialistic than in the United States. Custom and tradition in India demand that the buyer in the village should initiate the transaction. However, in the larger cities of many developing countries, particularly the rapidly developing nations of South Korea, Hong Kong and Thailand, there is an expanding demand creation industry. In these countries, particularly in the remote regions, lack of reliable media information limits the growth of the marketing communications industry. Multinational companies such as Singer (of sewing machine fame) operate throughout Thailand with a network of agents, lorries and posters subliminally conveying their marketing message.

A study in Sri Lanka showed that overall, approximately 80 per cent of all males and over half of the women were "reached" by at least one of the media studied. Illiteracy was lowest among urban men (4 per cent), and highest among rural women (42 per cent), and movie-going was a common habit in cities and towns. This kind of data was most useful in adapting marketing approaches to the population management campaign in Sri Lanka in the 1970s, when once again village halls, posters and samples and gifts were used widely and effectively to promote family planning systems.

The adaptation of advertising and sales promotional techniques from one nation to another is often carried out by a manufacturing and distribution firm expanding internationally. An example of this was the aggressive media (large-page) advertising by Sears Roebuck, when they moved into Mexico in 1947. These large advertisements, with drawings and prices, were innovators in this developing country. This policy has been pursued by Sears throughout Latin America.

Internationally mobile investment attracted to European countries has brought a sophistication to the advertising industry, often with American influences. Various laws and restrictions operate in many European countries. In the 1960s, German and French law restricted the type of message. An example was the Coca-Cola slogan of "refreshes you best" translated into over twenty languages, but the German agency was forced to substitute the more acceptable "refreshes you thoroughly".

Interesting variations between Europe and the United States were discussed in a study entitled *The European Approach to United States Markets*, by Professor James Ward, which included an investigation of product and promotion adaptation by multinational companies. The extent of adaptation by the fifty-two subsidiaries, where adaptations were made, and the use of standardised advertising were analysed. The major findings were as follows.

(*a*) Promotional adaptation was necessary in 71 per cent of the firms sampled.

(*b*) Adaptation was related to all aspects of the promotion mix. Four items in particular needed changing:

　(*i*) media used;
　(*ii*) sales incentives;
　(*iii*) volume of advertising; and
　(*iv*) distributor incentives.

(*c*) Standardised advertising was used by twenty-three companies (43 per cent of the sample).

(*d*) The nationality of the firm was a significant factor in the need for promotional adaptation and advertising standardisation. Continental firms did more promotion adaptation than British firms. In addition, 50 per cent of United Kingdom subsidiaries reported use of standardised advertisements, whereas only 17 per cent of the continentals did so. There were 27 United Kingdom and 25 continental firms in the total sample of 52.

Cultural attitudes to promotion vary between the United States and Europe, and vary within Europe between East and West and between EEC member states, and the international marketer should not underestimate promotion adaptation needs. It was not until the late 1950s that advertising and sales promotion developed in the USSR, when *Soviet Trade* and other periodicals began to accept advertising. However, progress was slow, and by 1965 only three national "Advertising Bureaux" were established. No great enthusiasm was shown by the retailers or the public.

In adapting the promotion effort to various export markets, therefore, it is important to consider the specific target market and its needs, the most appropriate channels of distribution in the host country, and the "state of the art" of marketing communications, together with local cultural norms.

SUMMARY

The marketing communications mix outlined in this chapter is based on a western industrialised nation setting, as this is where it has been developed and refined. However, with such a range of sophisticated mechanisms, it is important to be selective in terms of effectiveness and budget. In the context of export marketing, promotion adaptation is a further challenge in that the selected communication mix should be based on the value system, norms and "state of the advertising art" in the targeted export market.

QUESTIONS

1. As a future manager in British Leyland, outline an adapted promotion campaign for the Land Rover in any Third World country.

2. As an export manager for British Leyland, outline the adaptation of a promotion plan for the North American market for Land Rovers and Range Rovers.

CHAPTER THIRTEEN

Financing
Export Marketing

OBJECTIVES

In many decisions to seek out export markets, finance, its acquisition and disposal are central issues. As stated in earlier chapters, international marketing is part of an expansion and development plan which is meant to lead to greater profitability and financial strengthening. Yet, ironically, going international itself needs a stable financial base or well-planned economic financial acquisition arrangements. Successful marketers therefore understand the importance of the financial function as effective financial arrangements significantly strengthen competitive marketing positions. This chapter aims to provide a framework for such financial planning. The international marketer needs to know the financial objectives of his firm—both short-term and long-term—to ensure comprehensive export market planning. He also needs to know the firm's policy and legal restrictions on repatriation of profits or further re-investment possibilities in the export market.

VITAL NEED FOR FINANCE IN
EXPORT MARKET PLANNING

The key role of finance and international cash management is emphasised in various consulting models for optimal international market planning. For example, the Boston Consulting Group (BCG) model has cash flow and profitability through market share as part of its basic philosophy. This BCG model has been adapted and used in many firms and industries not just in the United States but world-wide. It is based on the need to show all international marketing operations in a comprehensive model. When a dynamic is incorporated, it is founded on the concept of the product life cycle which might apply to markets (i.e. markets often go through the development, growth, maturity and decline stages both generally and in regard to specific industries and products).

An outline is given in Fig. 27. Markets in the problem children segment are high growth markets, but the firm has low market share, so cash is needed for market development. South Korea (*SK*) is shown as such a market. Star markets are high growth areas with high market share, so are really healthy and need to be fostered. Two such markets are Japan (*J*) and Brazil (*B*). Germany (*G*) is in the cash cow segment which shows a high market share in a mature market. This means that cash is plentiful and should flow to help problem children to increase their market share. The United Kingdom (*UK*) is in the dog segment which means low market share in a low growth market. These markets may have to be phased out eventually. (*See also* Chapter 18.)

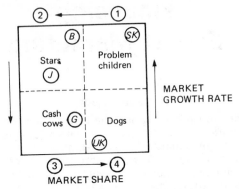

Fig. 27. *Boston Consulting Group for international market planning.*

It is important to note that all the markets have distinct needs in market planning and financial planning.

The financial demands of export marketing vary with the extent to which foreign participation is envisaged. For example, if there is a joint venture or if a foreign partner provides investment, less capital is needed by the exporting firm. If exclusive distribution rights are agreed with a foreign middleman, this may relieve the exporter of substantial direct costs and reduce the levels of risk and administration associated with marketing and distribution.

The *locus in quo* of financial decision-making can markedly affect operations, financial requirements and profitability, especially in times of monetary fluctuations. Decentralised or centralised cash management can both have advantages, depending on which perspective is used. The host nation and taxation often favour decentralisation, whereas economic uncertainty in corporate control favours centralisation.

Financial policy may vary between short-term and long-term profits and rate of return. As mentioned earlier, the United States often appears to demand a prompt rate of return, whereas the Japanese often put market share first in the first five years.

The financial requirements of international marketing are summarised in Fig. 28. In recent times the Japanese have found it advisable in Europe to promote *capital investment* in order to gain access to European markets. New start-up costs or extensive reorganisation may involve increased *overhead costs* on entering a new international market. Time lags and distance can cause a demand for increased *working capital* and this is often underestimated by new exporters. Greater *inventory costs* and greater management of these—often in various locations—can cause financial pressures on smaller exporters.

Channel and consumer credit is a key financing requirement for an export market, often because of local norms and inflation rates (e.g. Brazil 238 per cent, Argentina 700 per cent; Israel also is very high, currently over 400 per cent). In these circumstances, exporters may face up to a sixty-day turnaround.

Fig. 28. *Financial requirements of international marketing.*

The costs associated with *market penetration* can be formidable. They involve costs in building up channels and manpower, and apart from promotion and advertising, some distributors may have to be bought out, as happened to United States firms in Spain, Latin America, South Africa and Southern Europe. Existing distributors were bought out by competitors so United States firms had to do the same. Additional costs are often involved in *beating the competition* and building up market share; for example, special discounts and loss-making activities in the initial two or three years.

SOURCES OF FINANCE

There are many private and public sources for financing international business operations. These may be in the domestic country or in the overseas market, or indeed for large contracts involve international financing agencies such as the World Bank.

Many countries world-wide now place limits and restrictions on the outward movement of local capital to an overseas market. This is particularly, but not exclusively, true of developing countries. Ironically, there are at the same time many governments offering cash inducements in grants, tax exemption and various forms of financial incentives to entice investment from overseas. The United States multinationals manage huge investments overseas with, overall, less than 25 per cent through capital transfers from the United States. The Irish Industrial Development Authority's promotion in international finance journals claims that United States subsidiaries in Ireland were showing over 27 per cent return on investment. This claim in the early 1980s coincided with a world recession, when firms in many world markets were claiming to be doing well with 15 per cent rate of return.

Sources of finance for export marketing are outlined in Fig. 29. Private sources are still a popular method of raising finance. Companies with surpluses and joint ventures still provide substantial finance as equity holders. Various funding agencies, such as merchant bankers and commercial banks and overseas development banks, had rapid expansion phases in the 1970s, through playing a leading role in international finance.

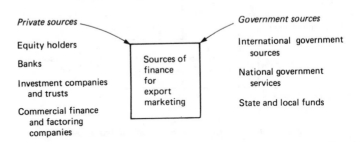

Fig. 29. *Sources of finance.*

Other funding institutions in the United States include investment companies and trusts and commercial finance and factoring companies. IBEC and ADELA are both multi-million-dollar United States investment companies financed by Rockefeller and top quality United States and European companies respectively.

Various national governments assist the financing of exports through their export and economic development agencies, often using industrial development and job promotion schemes (*see also* Chapter 19). International sources include the World Bank, the International Finance Corporation and the European Investment Bank.

CHALLENGES AND OPTIONS

The main aim in financing international marketing is to do so at the lowest possible cost, minimising the risks on international investments, exchanging foreign currencies, maintaining maximum flexibility including moving cash across national frontiers without exchange losses (and possibly with profits).

In all this, the firm will minimise competitive marketing advantages. World money markets are now truly international and through modern communications and computer systems, businessmen world-wide are actively using the international money markets, ranging through the European, Middle East, Japanese and United States markets. International funding management has become a highly skilled profession. Ability to finance purchases is still a very effective business-building, competitive operation. The organisation of payments in various currencies is also a major advantage when exchange rates fluctuate. Financing margins can equal or exceed trade margins, for example when United Kingdom exports to a Latin American country are paid for in German marks—all arranged through overnight telephone calls.

SUMMARY

In this chapter the importance of integrating finance (or international finance) with international marketing is emphasised. This integration is also evident in both funding and sourcing international finance. This chapter does not deal with pricing or the mechanics of collection/payment for exports as these topics are included in Chapters 14 and 16.

QUESTIONS

1. As a United Kingdom exporter of giftware to the United States, discuss the possible sources of funds to develop this export market.

2. As an export manager of India Ceramics, discuss the type of funding requirements to penetrate a market of an EEC member state.

CHAPTER FOURTEEN

The Logistics of Exporting

OBJECTIVES

This chapter aims to outline relevant factors and ask key questions regarding the organisation of optimum cash flow, insurance and transportation/packing systems. As there is no single correct system for all industries and markets, a descriptive mechanistic approach is avoided. However, this whole area of procedures and documentation should not be underestimated in importance, but can best be understood in skill terms by actually *doing*. This is sometimes possible through practice projects in groups, or by joining the exporting department of an effective international marketing organisation for a brief training period.

PAYMENT/COLLECTION MECHANISMS

The extent to which the exporter becomes involved in cash transfer mechanisms across national boundaries is dependent on whether there is an intermediary involved who undertakes these on behalf of the exporter. Regulations and restrictions of both the source country and the target market can impact on exporting and export payments. In many countries, there is a requirement for both export and import licences. Customs duties, exchange permits and quotas all require documentation procedures, as do health, sanitation and packaging regulations. In many cases, export agents and free trade zones can simplify much of these procedures and documentation. These zones include freeports, transit zones and other special facilities, mainly concerned with customs-privileged facilities. There are several hundred world-wide, in both the industrialised world and developing countries. In the United States alone, the volume of trade moving through free trade zones now exceeds 2 billion dollars annually. In the last five years, thirty-three new trade zones have been established in the United States, compared to eighteen in the previous forty years. (*See also* Chapter 21.)

Payments for exports are complicated by risks of non-payment, costs of collection, exchange control, distance and differing legal systems. These may be minimised by letters of credit, commercial dollar or sterling drafts or bills of exchange drawn by the seller on the buyer, and sometimes by open accounts with cash payments in advance.

Pre-shipment financing is most important for small-scale exporters. However, post-shipment financing is more commonly arranged through:

(*a*) commercial banks;

(b) banks linked to an export credit insurance service;
(c) merchant banks;
(d) insurance companies;
(e) other financial institutions.

Loans may be short, medium or long term. Table V summarises the methods of payment.

TABLE V. METHODS OF PAYMENT IN EXPORTING

Type of payment	When you get your money	Extent of risk☆
Cash payment	With the order	No risk
Open account	Specified time after delivery to customer	Risk of total loss if customer fails to pay
Shipment on consignment	After customer has resold the goods	Risk of loss if customer fails to sell the goods
Documentary credit using letter of credit	At time of shipment	Risk limited to cost of bringing back goods from your port
Documentary collection using paid bill of exchange or sight draft	On arrival at port of destination	Risk of having to bring back goods or dispose of them at a loss
Documentary collection using accepted bill of exchange or time draft	Specified time after delivery to customer	Risk of total loss if customer dishonours bill of exchange with the bank

☆Less risk if you have an export credit guarantee arrangement with your government.

INSURANCE SYSTEMS AND CREDIT MANAGEMENT

An export credit guarantee scheme is offered by many governments to minimise risk and to encourage exports. The British Export Credits Guarantee Department (ECGD) is responsible to the Secretary of State for Trade and Industry. It has nine regional offices in addition to its London head office. The ECGD offers two main services:

(a) insurance cover for non-payment by overseas customers;
(b) guarantees to banks for firms to gain finance for export credit transactions, often at favourable interest rates.

In a recent year, over 10,500 exporters insured their overseas business with the ECGD to a total value of some £19,000 million—over a third of all visible non-oil exports. The *average* premium is about 60p per £100 insured. (*See also* Chapter 19.)

Other insurance systems are necessary for safety in transportation, and are dealt with later in this chapter.

Credit management in export marketing has an important impact on cash flow. Credit policy will be affected by a range of factors, as shown in Fig. 30.

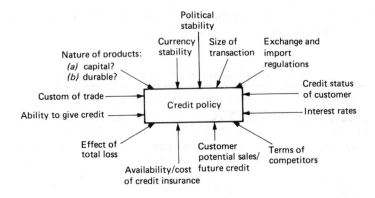

Fig. 30. *Factors affecting credit.*

Checking the creditworthiness of a customer is often difficult in an export market. Some guidance may be obtained from:

(a) your agent in a foreign country;
(b) your bank (to bank in a foreign country);
(c) a credit-rating organisation (e.g. Dun and Bradstreet);
(d) a fellow export marketer already operating in the target market (this can be valuable, although unofficial).

The following key questions may be helpful for customer credit.

(a) What is the risk of total loss?
(b) Can we insure against loss?
(c) How long will the debt be outstanding?
(d) What else could we do with the money for that period?
(e) Can we finance the credit?
(f) What will the customer do if we say no?
(g) How important is this order to us?
(h) What is the future potential of the customer?

In credit management, it is important to have an excellent agent, or know your target market, and get to know your customer.

TRANSPORTATION

In the majority of cases, geography, availability of services and the physical characteristics of the product are factors which influence the exporter in choosing a transportation system. This choice will in turn determine to a certain extent the selection of the packing system for safety and the logistics of handling and storage.

There have been rapid advances in world transportation systems, with East/West and North/South airways competing keenly with shipping. Europe is still very much at the centre of the system, as shown in Fig. 31.

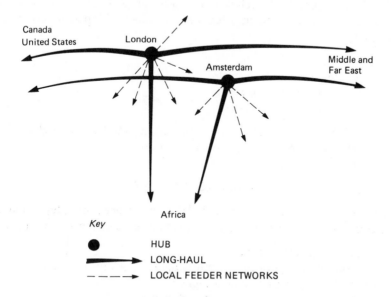

Fig. 31. *Some world air transport networks.*

International marketing between inter-continental markets and between developing and industrialised nations essentially means a choice between air and sea transport, and air transport is increasing its share of world trade. It is interesting to note the growing number of free trade zones or freeports located at international airports. (It should also be noted that three out of the six new United Kingdom freeports designated in 1984 are located at airports.) This is probably due to the improved systems and economics of air transportation, the growth in international assemblies of high technology components, and the higher standards of service and urgency of the affluent industrialised countries.

Road and rail may be used for exports to countries on the same continent. In developing countries, road and rail transport are basically for moving goods to and from docks or airports.

Ocean freight is still the most widely used form of transportation in international trade. It has cost attractions for moving large quantities of goods (particularly bulky products) over large distances. Only large exporters handle their own shipping documentation. Smaller exporters use forwarding agents, or freight forwarders, for booking space, arranging documentation and often collecting goods at the factory and delivering to the docks or airport. Agents also arrange payments and often consolidate a number of consignments involving the booking of containers at economic prices.

Air freight has many advantages for products with a high unit value, i.e. a high ratio of price to weight. The obvious advantage is speed of delivery, e.g. when flying in fresh orchids to London from Asia, or fresh fruits from South America. Cost savings for many products shipped by air freight include:

(a) lower inventory costs;
(b) greater security in transit;
(c) less jostling in transit;
(d) lower insurance costs.

Air freight procedures are more modern and simpler, although in many cases the small exporter will use an air cargo agent.

PACKING SYSTEMS

Packing systems tend to vary, as do cargo insurance costs, depending on the transportation system. Factors affecting the packing system include:

(a) product characteristics;
(b) mode of transportation (much lighter packing is needed for the expensive but more careful air freight);
(c) climatic conditions encountered during the journey;
(d) customers' requirements;
(e) government regulations.

Commodity products have special packing and labelling requirements. The packing system selected has to strike a balance between providing:

(a) a case strong enough to withstand transportation hazards, e.g. rough handling, pilfering, crushing and corrosion; and
(b) a case which is light and compact enough to keep freight charges down.

CARGO INSURANCE

One of the better known insurance systems is marine insurance, with various types of cover. Normally specific risks are listed in the policies. The following are the main systems.

(a) FPA (free of particular average) is the minimal coverage in general use. It covers losses if a ship or an aircraft is totally lost.
(b) WPA (with particular average) insures against goods being damaged in transit.
(c) "All risks" insures against all risks except war, unless this has been specified.

This is a highly specialised subject, and an insurance broker should be used as a consultant when deciding what insurance is prudent.

SUMMARY

This chapter has attempted to give an appreciation of a range of important aspects in the organisation of export marketing. In areas such as freighting systems, documentation and optimum cash flows, it is best to consult specialist agents or the specialist export financing department of a bank. This is also true for insurance and packing systems, as this enables the exporter to concentrate on what he should know best—the production of the goods or services and personal contact with his customer and/or agent.

QUESTIONS

1. As shipping manager, you must decide between air and sea shipment for the consignments listed in the table below. Your company pays 12 per cent per annum for its working capital requirements, and all the consignments are due to be paid for on documentary sight terms on arrival at final destination.

Air freight takes twenty-four hours to reach the final destination. Sea transportation with the necessary land links takes two months on average.

Calculate the total cost of sea transport. Compare this with the air freight cost. Which method of transport would you recommend for each consignment? What additional information might you need in each case to assist you in making a decision?

Item	Value	Ocean freight cost	Extra packing for ocean freight	Air freight cost
	£	£	£	£
Shoes	5,000	200	100	1,000
Transistor radios	50,000	200	100	1,200
Tractor	10,000	600	50	4,000
Fresh-cut flowers	500	200	50	600
Tinned mangoes	100	100	none	200
Publicity material	500	100	none	500
Hand-made jewellery	10,000	100	75	350
Hammers	8,000	2,000	none	20,000

2. As a potential management consultant, advise the Thai producers of fresh flowers (orchids) on the rationale for flying rather than shipping their produce to London daily.

CHAPTER FIFTEEN

Agency and Distribution Policy in the Foreign Market

OBJECTIVES

This chapter aims to provide the reader with an understanding of alternative approaches to agency and distribution policy determination, by discussing the range of perspectives offered by various writers.

WHAT IS DISTRIBUTION?

Distribution might be defined as the management activity of a firm concerned with the provision of availability, where the view is held that the channels of distribution are legal entities which take possession and title to goods as they move from producer to consumer. Weinstein and Fargher comment, however, that this traditional concept is grossly over-simplified, and go on to state that more modern management theorists view channels of distribution as systems. Systems thinking has been applied to distribution to a greater extent than any other aspect of marketing behaviour and management. The strength of this approach is that it illustrates that the channels of distribution can be managed and are flexible enough to change within the current turbulent environment.

The latter issue is of paramount importance, as it is essential that strategic priorities are focused on the provision of an effective distribution policy.

ANALYSIS AND AUDIT

Stern and El Ansary propound that there is a myriad of inter-organisational problems associated with international marketing, and this point is also emphasised by Bickers, who comments that the mere fact of operating in a foreign market introduces complexity to a company. This fact should not be a deterrent, but merely act as a warning. Having identified the existence of a lucrative market abroad, strategic decisions must be formulated on an analytical, systematic basis in order to minimise risks.

For the purposes of this chapter, it is assumed that the companies intending to enter foreign markets have adopted the marketing concept— that is, the provision of consumer needs in relation to the achievement of company objectives. In order then to formulate a distribution policy, an audit should be undertaken in relation to product, consumer, corporate capabilities and external environment. This can be summarised as follows.

(*a*) *Product characteristics.* Unit value (for example, products with a high unit value usually tend towards direct channels), perishability, fashion, standardisation, stage of market development, length and breadth of product line, technical nature of product.

(*b*) *Consumers.* All socio-economic data is required about consumers, e.g. frequency of purchase, number and product use.

(*c*) *Company resources.* Including financial strength, reputation, objectives and policies, structure and organisation.

(*d*) *External environment.* Competition characteristics, economic climate, legal and government issues, social and cultural values.

For a more detailed exposition on the above, see Weinstein and Fargher, or Channon.

CHANGING CONDITIONS IN THE EXPORT MARKET-PLACE

Before discussing distribution policy, it is important to note that in this respect there are two interactive systems, as shown in Fig. 32.

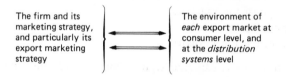

Fig. 32. *Interactive systems affecting distribution policy.*

Distribution strategy "emerges" from an analysis of those interactions. It is important to note that each export market may be quite distinct and that there are two levels at which change should be observed—the consumer and distribution system levels.

The principal contribution of distribution is in providing time and place utility. However, retailing, wholesaling and transportation account for well over 50 per cent of the total marketing cost, and for substantial employment in most western economies.

DISTRIBUTION POLICY AND EVALUATION
OF ALTERNATIVE APPROACHES

As emphasised earlier, distribution policy is just one aspect of marketing policy. Distribution policy will depend to some extent on whether the firm has adopted a *push* (on the channels) or *pull* (by the consumers) strategy. This in turn depends to some extent on which stage the product or service is at in the product life cycle: development, growth, maturity or decline.

Level, type and number

Leighton argues that there are three main aspects to distribution policy:

(*a*) selecting the *level* at which to sell;
(*b*) selecting the *type* of distribution organisation to which to sell;
(*c*) selecting the *number* of distribution organisations to which to sell.

In terms of *level*, there is generally a more direct approach with industrial products. However, with consumer goods such as food there may be two or three distribution levels, before it reaches the final consumer. Policy will tend to take account of the following factors:

(*a*) size of potential market;
(*b*) political and social factors, including legislation;
(*c*) economics of distribution;
(*d*) intensity of promotion effort needed.

Examples of changes in *type* selected include traditional household health products sold through chemists, which are now often sold through retail food chains.

In determining the *number* of outlets, consideration might be given to:

(*a*) the buying habits of customers;
(*b*) coverage of the market;
(*c*) selling support needed;
(*d*) the competition network.

The question of exclusive distributorships is often decided by the bargaining position of the parties. A strong manufacturer and good product can exert pressure on the distributor.

Such an analysis of level, type and number is a useful framework for an audit or general review of existing distribution policies.

Developing a strategy

Having accomplished a distribution audit, the channel analyst is enabled to commence formulating a distribution strategy for evaluation within the following framework of goals, as expounded by Stern.

(*a*) to achieve adequate market coverage;
(*b*) to maintain control over goods in the channel;
(*c*) to hold distribution costs to reasonable levels;
(*d*) to ensure the continuity of channel relationships, and consequently continuous presence in the market;
(*e*) to achieve marketing goals expressed in terms of volume, market share, margin requirements and return on investment.

Guirdham summarises an approach to channel strategy as follows:

(*a*) channel selection;

(*b*) selection of intermediaries and the development of policies regarding them;

(*c*) persuasion of the selected intermediaries to participate in the channel;

(*d*) channel administration and improvement of performance;

(*e*) provision of resources and organisation for channel functions not delegated to intermediaries;

(*f*) the devising and operation of information and control systems in order to ensure channel effectiveness.

However, before any resultant policies can be structured, choice has to be made between fundamentally different alternatives, namely whether to:

(*a*) extend the duties of the domestic company to embrace overseas operations; or

(*b*) create a specialist international company division or department.

CHANNELS OF DISTRIBUTION

It is essential to note at the outset that it is virtually impossible to generalise categorically about international marketing channels, because, as Stern comments, there are vast environmental differences between countries (*see* Fig. 33). He, among others, contends that there are four basic routes to expansion overseas, as follows.

(*a*) *Exportation:* through the use of foreign distributors or agents, or by establishing overseas marketing subsidiaries.

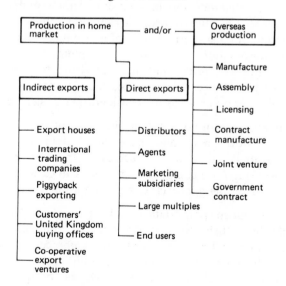

Fig. 33. *Distribution channels.*

(b) *Licensing:* whereby the company forges a contractual agreement with a foreign organisation to manufacture and/or sell its products abroad within an agreement apropos the apportionment of profit; for example, Pilkington's float glass which is made under licence by many foreign manufacturers, or the Coca-Cola company franchise.

(c) *Joint ventures:* where two or more firms share the venture and thus the risk of the expansionary effort; for example, Dupont.

(d) *Direct investment:* where the home company aims to maintain a high degree of control over the marketing of its products abroad, and thus establishes a wholly-owned subsidiary in a foreign market; for example, Philips and Nestlés.

Exporting—both directly and indirectly

Indirect exporting is the most popular method for an organisation which is commencing to market on a global scale, as less investment and risk are involved. Because the producer employs international marketing middle-men, he has the benefit of their specialist knowledge and experience of the particular market under review, and consequently should make fewer mistakes. Within this framework, there are some alternatives, although Frain propounds that some theorists do not make any distinction between distributors and agents.

The company can choose to appoint a commission agent: the main feature of this method of exporting is that the agent does not normally hold stocks, but passes on orders to the principals, taking for his efforts 5 or 10 per cent commission. These agents are usually employed in small or little developed territories. Chisnall notes they can be either shared or exclusive, but warns that their appointment should not be undertaken lightly. He propounds that exhaustive enquiries should be made into their commercial standing, and suggests that careful attention should be directed towards the formulation of the trade agreement with respect to, for example, commission, prices and discount structure, methods of promotion, provision of after-sales service, and duration of agency agreement. However, two key areas for consideration in agent selection are:

(a) the importance of compatibility in terms of know-how, range of existing agency work, image and operational system; and

(b) the possibility of conflict of interest in that the best agents may already be working for a competitor, and this can cause a rethink in the selection, and even the approach to representation.

It is essential that an appropriate agent is chosen. Government agencies, for example the British Overseas Trade Board, commercial attachés at British Embassies and local chambers of commerce, can offer specific facilities and information to companies requiring assistance in choice. There are many particular types of agents who can be appointed. Briefly, they are:

(*a*) a commission agent, who does not hold stock or provide after-sales service;

(*b*) a stocking agent, who provides storage and handling, but who does not take title to the goods;

(*c*) an agent who provides full service, and in addition to the above, offers after-sales service; and

(*d*) a *del credere* agent, who accepts the credit risk involved, but who requests a higher rate of commission.

At a strategic level, it is the responsibility of the organisation to assess the agent's suitability for the specific marketing tasks to be accomplished and to control his work by monitoring progress in accordance with agreed targets. Bickers notes that agents with specialist knowledge skills are employed by manufacturers of expensive equipment, e.g. aircraft, power plants, armaments and other military equipment.

Another mode open to the organisation is through the use of independent distributors, who maintain stocks, thus investing their own capital, and do not involve the manufacturer beyond the agreed credit period. The distributors market the goods themselves, on their own terms, and have a considerable incentive to sell enthusiastically, thus providing a more motivated sales force with well-established contacts.

The major disadvantage inherent in this method is that, as the distributors are autonomous and independent, they retain power in the structure of pricing decisions, promotional policies and general marketing issues. Efficient distributors have a depth of knowledge about the products they handle, and the producer should ensure that they receive an adequate briefing. Some goods, for example well-established consumer lines, sell effectively with little effort on the part of the distributor, whereas others, for example light engineering goods, require specialist knowledge and this results in difficulties in obtaining satisfactory distributors. Alternative strategies then need to be formulated.

Overseas branch or subsidiary
An alternative policy is for the organisation to set up an overseas branch or subsidiary company. However, this has some disadvantages—the greatest of these being, according to Bickers, the burden of solitude, i.e. attempting to cope with the intricacies of national laws and regulations, dealing with an alien culture and bearing all the other problems of establishing a new venture unaided. Heavy financial risks must also be taken. The main advantage of this mode of expansion is unification. There is little potential for conflict as all personnel are employed exclusively for the same company: effective established working practices and standardisation of systems and methods can be applied to the new market, all accruing profits do not have to be divided and in behavioural terms, it may be easier internally to deal with known colleagues.

Joint ventures

The implications and full significance of forming joint ventures overseas with an indigenous organisation must be appreciated. Bickers states that the consequences may be far-reaching and enduring and therefore need careful systematic analysis before such a decision is taken. However, it should be noted that legal requirements in some countries necessitate the construction of joint ventures, as it is not legally possible to set up an operation which is wholly owned by a foreign firm.

Joint venturing differs from exporting, according to Kotler, in that it involves partnership which leads to the establishment of some production facilities abroad, and it differs from direct investment in that an association is formed with someone in that country. The following four types of joint ventures can be distinguished.

(*a*) *Licensing:* where the licenser enters an agreement with a licensee in a foreign market offering the right to use a manufacturing process, trademark or patent for a fee or royalty. The licenser gains entry into the market with very little risk and the licensee acquires production expertise or a well-known name without having to go through the initial stages.

(*b*) *Contract manufacturing:* where the organisation may retain marketing responsibility, but does not wish to acquire foreign production facilities. Local manufacturers thus produce the article but the main disadvantage is that the original company has less control over the production function and loses profits on manufacturing.

(*c*) *Management contracting:* a low risk method of obtaining a foothold in international markets. The domestic firm exports management services rather than its own products and supplies management expertise to a foreign company which supplies capital.

(*d*) *Joint ownership ventures:* where foreign investors join with local investors to establish a local business in which joint ownership and control are shared. This may be necessary for political or economic reasons. Certain disadvantages may be that there may be disagreement or conflict over policies. Some governments insist that the local partner has the controlling share, and this is not always acceptable to investing companies.

Direct investment

The final method of becoming involved in international markets is by direct investment. Kotler comments that companies commencing to market abroad should avoid this alternative, initially because of the inherent risks and the considerable amount of capital expenditure.

Thus, as Chisnall notes, the decision should only be taken after thorough research into all factors affecting production has been carried out. Such factors include: employment policies of the country under review, external constraints (political and economic) and the recruitment and training of a suitable work-force.

MONITORING PERFORMANCE

Standards of performance can only be measured properly when there are specific aims and objectives for the distribution channels in the first place. This task is often overlooked, and yet it can provide vital feedback. One exception is the motor car industry, where market share is regularly monitored. In this industry, there is also measurement against the potential of the market and performance of previous years. Prizes are awarded annually to dealers on a national and regional basis; this is accompanied by a range of editorial and other public relations follow-ups.

Apart from sales volume, other measures of interest include repeat business (product loyalty) and new business development (new customers or market segmentation), number, quality and areas of displays, and percentage out of stock.

In addition to actual performance, factors such as salesmen's reports, public surveys and other research agency reports can give vital feedback.

SELECTION OF AGENTS AND DISTRIBUTORS

Agency selection is a critical area which affects the whole development of the export effort. The main challenge is to select and appoint an agent who knows the export market and has influence with the key buying personnel in the appropriate sectors, and knows and is committed to your business.

A preliminary list should be drawn up with the assistance of exporters, embassy or export promotion agency offices abroad, or through friends or local chambers of commerce and banks.

The next step is to write to the organisations and industrialists on this list, giving your firm's background and export objectives, and checking if they are interested in handling your products and services, whether they act for competitors in that market, and their terms of commission.

The replies received give the basis of a short list, which in turn is the basis for interviews when you next visit the market with a *local* export adviser/*local* banker. Trade and banker's references can then be taken up and an appointment made.

SUMMARY

In this chapter, use has been made of a wide range of perspectives with many authors quoted. This can form the basis for further reading; as this area is vast and very important. However, this approach is balanced by the systematic guidelines for planning distribution activities, monitoring and evaluating them, together with a procedure for rigorous agent selection which is a critical aspect of distribution policy implementation.

QUESTIONS

1. As a potential export manager, develop and discuss a checklist of criteria for agency selection.

2. As a United Kingdom food manufacturer, outline your distribution policy for exporting your cheese to the German market.

CHAPTER SIXTEEN

Pricing Plans for Export Market Penetration

OBJECTIVES

This chapter aims to give the reader an insight into pricing policy for planning for export market penetration. Pricing is one of the most critical aspects of the marketing mix and yet it can only be undertaken after all the other aspects of marketing have been investigated. This is essentially because the product, presentation, packaging, promotion and distribution will all impact on price in terms of cost "push". Pricing must also await the market, and competitor investigation in terms of demand "pull" or "what the market will bear". So it can be seen that pricing policy and pricing is crucial to the success or failure of all our export marketing efforts. A poorly set price can deprive the firm of the funds to do an effective market development job and thus yield a return on investment.

SOME PRICING POLICY ISSUES

As mentioned earlier, pricing policy can be directly related to business policy in general, and specifically export marketing policy. For example, it has been shown that some Japanese firms have a policy of gaining a high market share in the first five years, and later emphasising the rate of return on investment. This approach can affect their pricing policy and their promotion budget during the early years, during which they project a quality product at a reasonable price in a "value for money" image build-up. Then they can ease up their margins of profit *gradually* through:

(*a*) greater volume and a position of strength (market share and image);
(*b*) slightly reduced promotion budget; and
(*c*) slightly higher prices (gradually eased up through years 3 to 5).

The decision on what price to set for a product will have to take into account:

(*a*) the market;
(*b*) the costs to the exporter;
(*c*) the competition;
(*d*) the intended profit margin.

A systematic questioning, as outlined below, will help to clear the exporter's mind in setting an export price at the appropriate level.

(*a*) How will total demand and demand for the specific product respond to price changes? Will a lower price induce more people to buy more of the product or is demand not sensitive to price?
(*b*) How will the competition react if the price is lowered?

(c) Can profits be maximised by selling a large quantity at a low price or selling a smaller quantity at a higher price?

(d) Will an initial low price be an effective means of gaining a foothold in the market which will not easily be dislodged?

(e) Will lower prices give an image of lower quality and service?

(f) Would it be wise to "skim" the market by charging high prices at the beginning and then reducing when the enthusiastic minority have bought and as competitors move in?

(g) How can prices impact on the product in the longer term when the market is saturated?

(h) Is the market best penetrated by high prices and high marketing expenditure or low prices and a minimum of service?

Figure 34 summarises the three main influences on pricing policy:

Fig. 34. *Influences on pricing.*

(a) market;
(b) competition;
(c) costs.

The cost structure is built up from the usual domestic cost elements of raw materials, labour, overheads of factory and administration, together with selling and distribution costs. The additional costs of exporting include transport, insurance, agents' margins and overseas promotion costs. There is also the need to allow for currency fluctuations in costing and pricing for international markets.

MARGINAL COSTING AND PRICING

The greater volume sales which successful exporting ensures can mean a greater spread of overheads and lower unit costs. It is important to note this interaction of volume impact on costs, and costs in turn impacting on price, which in turn at lower levels can increase volume sales. This is shown in Fig. 35.

Fig. 35 *Cost/price/volume interaction.*

Some exporters worry that the price in a particular export market is less than the domestic market and that they will have to export at a loss. However, this is not always the case, as exporting can be profitable even when prices are lower.

The exporter's costs include labour, materials and overheads, but there are also selling and delivery costs—often major items in exporting. As mentioned earlier, as volume increases, unit costs are reduced when produced within the same fixed costs framework (factory, rent, machinery, manager's salary). Let us say that fixed costs are £1,000: for a production of 1,000, each will bear £1 costs. However, for an additional 1,000 export order, the fixed costs of £1,000 are spread over 2,000 products, or 50p per unit. If the variable cost of each product is £4, the total *unit* cost with domestic sales of 1,000 is £5, but when the additional export sales are produced at the same unit variable cost of £4, the total *unit* cost in producing 2,000 products is £4.50 or an additional margin of £500, which can be used to offset the additional export selling and distribution costs.

The key to marginal costing is to view domestic sales and export sales as separate compartments, and to consider export sales as "extra" sales. This is not so strange, because in the recession of the early 1980s many small and medium-sized businesses have seen their domestic sales dwindle to a point where they are operating at 40 or 50 per cent capacity, and in some cases less. This means factory rent, machinery and factory manager (fixed costs) have to be paid for, and 50–60 per cent spare capacity is available for export market development. If the exporter is recovering fixed costs on home sales, he can consider the extra costs of the products for export to be the variable costs (including export selling and distribution costs). However, the break-even for exports can be far lower than if the calculation were on the basis of both fixed and variable costs. The difference is indicated by the space between the dotted and solid lines in Fig. 36. It is important to note that marginal costing is valid only if there is *no additional investment in factory, plant and machinery for export production.*

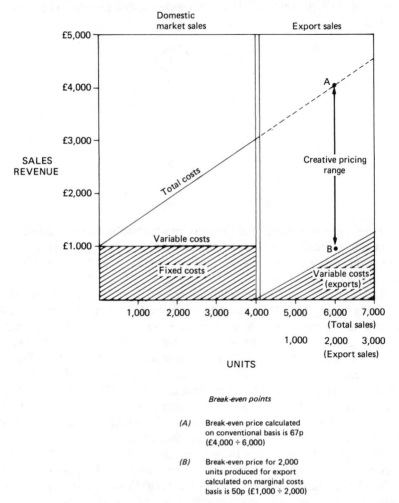

Fig. 36. *Costs and creative pricing for exports.*

In terms of initial penetration impact, the key to calculating export costs, in order to see how low prices can be cut, is to look at marginal costs.

However, marginal costing is probably best used, not to lower export prices—at least not *too low* or for *too long*—but to justify higher expenditure on marketing and promotion.

It should be emphasised that there are pitfalls in longer-term marginal cost pricing for exports. One is that in the longer term, and for larger orders, the domestic market-based fixed costs may become inadequate through extensions to buildings, new plant, and extended overhead budgets. Therefore, the momentum of successful exporting will soon build up a need for its own fixed costs, and prices may very soon be found to be inadequate. An additional hazard to marginal cost pricing is the range of anti-dumping legislation in various parts of the world.

CREATIVE PRICING

The concept of creative pricing was introduced in Fig. 36. Creative pricing means taking advantage of the flexibility between the lower limit of the break-even price and the upper limit of the competitors' price for similar products.

Very often, marginal costs are so low that they give the exporter great scope for aggressive pricing policies, or for heavy expenditure on initial and continuing promotion, or for absorbing the extra costs involved in exporting. Generally, the more successful exporting firm is able to set a price higher than the lowest in the market place, because its product has perceived higher values. These can include:

(*a*) a good reputation, resulting from successful promotion;

(*b*) effective and attractive packaging;

(*c*) reliable quality and service; and

(*d*) excellent service from the more reputable retailers and wholesalers.

Pricing is only one element, but a critical one in building up this export marketing position.

SUMMARY

Pricing strategy has its roots in the firm's overall strategy and should be consistent with the other elements in the export promotion plan. It is important to understand the range of complex factors, both inside and outside the firm, which will influence pricing policy. Although the role and potential of marginal costing for export pricing should be clearly understood, its limitations and shortcomings should also be studied. Creative pricing is the area that calls on the skills and judgment of the innovative international marketer.

QUESTIONS

1. As a potential export manager, advise a Third World exporter on the limitations of a cost-plus approach to export pricing.

2. As a motor car exporter, how would you analyse the pricing policy for Jaguar cars in the Middle East market.

CHAPTER SEVENTEEN

Management and Staff Development

OBJECTIVES

This chapter aims to give the reader an understanding of:
(a) the key role of the manager and the management team in successful export marketing; and
(b) the importance of having a management structure and management and staff development policy to meet the challenges in international marketing.

THE HUMAN FACTOR

Meeting the challenges already discussed in relation to the firm's entry into and further development in international marketing is only possible through the vision, initiative and total commitment of *people* at owner/manager and staff team level. Of all aspects of business, international marketing calls for the greatest enterprise, imagination and endeavour. This is recognised: risks are often greater and there is the element of venturing into the unknown—location, climate, culture, language and currency. All of these can be formidable barriers to the faint-hearted. Yet the merchant adventurers of past centuries traded across the Indian Ocean and around the Eurasian landmass, contending with much greater hazards than does today's telex and satellite communicating, jet-setting international marketer. In this chapter, it is proposed to deal with this central cell of energy and drive—the human factor, and its mobilisation, motivation and leadership.

KEY ROLE OF MANAGEMENT AND STAFF

In their best-selling book *In Search of Excellence*, Peters and Waterman highlight key factors which mark out the truly professionally managed and successful enterprise. These might be briefly summarised under three main headings, which are most applicable to successful international marketing:

(a) innovation and constant creativity (not just one week each year, but every day);
(b) closeness to the customers, knowing and providing for their needs; and
(c) mobilising the whole organisation in a similar manner to provide a flexible and responsive organisation.

These are key traits for success in international marketing, as the scope and challenges demand such innovativeness and creativity, not just in the owner and managers, but in the whole staff team.

Knowing and staying close to the international customer can be even more challenging than dealing with the domestic customer, who is more accessible. All the earlier points on product adaptation and packaging, together with understanding the local cultural value system and buying behaviour, can be effectively achieved only through knowing the customer well.

Motivating and mobilising the whole organisation to be flexible and responsive to international market needs is also a challenging task, as the majority may never have been in the particular international market. Various methods can be used to try to achieve this team approach to export priorities:

(a) despatch of key managers and supervisors to the international market-place;

(b) inviting key buyers from overseas to meet the work-force in the domestic production centre; and

(c) discussing with staff teams the culture, value system and priorities of the overseas customers, using if possible videos and taped discussion on product specifications.

The key role of owners and managers is to investigate and interpret the needs of the international market, adapt the product to meet these needs, and communicate with and motivate the production and marketing teams to develop and market the product. The staff team's role is to be flexible and adaptable to meet the market needs to ensure customer satisfaction and the market penetration which follows.

MANAGEMENT STRUCTURE

At the export start-up stage, management structure questions will include the following.

(a) Is the owner or chief executive fully committed, and will there be an involvement by the board?

(b) Has the person with board level responsibility got the competence as well as the commitment for developing international markets?

(c) Is there a well-qualified deputy for international market negotiations?

(d) Is there a sound management team back-up to maintain and develop the domestic market?

(e) Is there a sound management team in the marketing and distribution agency with which the firm is dealing in the target market?

(f) Has the production manager and team been fully involved and informed through visits to the target market?

(g) Is the finance manager fully briefed on export financing?

All these questions are relevant to the smaller firm of up to 100 employees, and to medium-sized firms who have no export experience.

For companies already in exporting who wish to expand, and for larger companies, more detailed management structure questions might arise, depending on whether they are undertaking the range of international marketing functions. In many cases where overseas agents or domestic export houses are used, many larger firms do not need a complicated management and staff structure for exporting, and a simple structure of two or three key individuals will suffice.

However, where the main international marketing functions are undertaken, various manpower needs have to be assessed:

(a) policy/management structure for export marketing based in the home office;
(b) temporary support staff based at the home office;
(c) marketing managers based overseas; and
(d) overseas sales force.

One possible structure which is quite widely used, and which can be adapted to various industrial sector needs, is based on centralised marketing functions, but decentralised sales staff, i.e. staying close to the customer (see Fig. 37). This approach allows for detailed knowledge of each country and market in critical areas, while drawing on head office for support functions such as market research and sales promotion.

The main challenge in management structuring is to maintain a flexible structure which will be sensitive and relevant to the needs attendant on successful exporting.

TRAINING AND DEVELOPMENT

Any worthwhile management development policy for an international marketing firm should be rooted in a rigorous management training needs analysis. This is outlined in Fig. 38.

A comprehensive management training needs analysis should start with the board, its chairman and chief executive, or in the smaller firm the owner(s) and the board. At this level the role of each constituent party should be clarified. Some strategy formulation workshops, particularly international marketing strategy sessions, may be required. Any gaps in board expertise might be filled by non-executive appointments. The next step would be to analyse the main competencies required for the senior and middle management teams in developing and implementing the export marketing plan. These will include international marketing research, product and possible production systems adaptation, export finance, export promotion and export sales management. The existing team and *its*

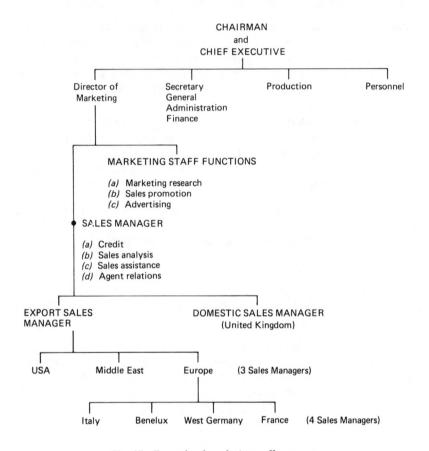

Fig. 37. *Example of marketing staff structure.*

potential is then assessed against required standards of attitude knowledge and skills schedules, and a management development policy and plan is developed.

The process of implementing management development plans might include a range of facets—process/method (such as team-building action sets), on-site/off-site development projects and courses, and case study and other learning materials, preferably pertinent to the industry and the target market. In respect to the latter, self-learning, interactive micro-systems are an exciting and rapidly developing facility. This process should include a comprehensive review of management development agencies, including a careful evaluation of two or three alternatives before a selection is made. It is often useful to include the local consultant or college selected in the review of the policy and plan, as this can lead to more precision in establishing management training objectives and the design of development processes and programmes, and their evaluation/review.

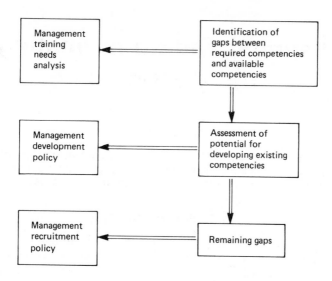

Fig. 38. *Management development scheme.*

SUMMARY

In this chapter, the importance of the "human factor" has been stressed. It plays a vital part in energising the whole process of international marketing, including the key areas of creativity, imagination and flair. This combination, when considered with enthusiasm and the promotion of the excitement factor, as well as the hard work and commitment factors, is the chemistry which stimulates the whole firm to excellence in performance and quality in international marketing. This human factor, of course, must be constantly updated for the rapidly changing challenges and opportunities of the international market-place.

QUESTIONS

1. As a potential UK exporter of food products to the French market, how would you organise and develop your management structure?

2. What management development processes and agencies might you consider for an existing export management team in the London area?

CHAPTER EIGHTEEN

Planning and Co-ordinating the Operations

OBJECTIVES

This chapter aims to provide the reader with an insight into the importance of systematically approaching the planning and co-ordination of international marketing operations, and the factors relevant to this process.

NEED FOR FLEXIBILITY

In dealing with topics such as planning and co-ordinating it is easy to slip into an emphasis on control systems and bureaucratic monitoring procedures. This emphasis is even more likely when the previous chapter on management and organisation structures is referred to. However, it would be unfortunate if planning and co-ordinating international marketing operations did not take into account the need for flexibility and sensitivity to rapid intra-market as well as inter-market changes. From the early chapters of this book it will be seen that many and rapid changes take place in terms of the diverse markets themselves, the political and legal environments, transportation and distribution systems and competitive positions regarding prices and product quality. In fact, the firm may not find it feasible to have one standard planning and co-ordinating system, but needs a number with adaptations to different market conditions. The challenge is to manage this tension between control and flexibility, between one system and too many diverse systems.

It may be worth identifying an example of where flexibility was found to be important. Hulbert and Brandt undertook some research in Brazil in the 1970s, in which the marketing strategies of subsidiaries of European, Japanese and United States firms were examined and quite distinct approaches noted. The Japanese had a market penetration objective in the first five years which gave greatest flexibility in tendering and immediate decision-making, whereas the United States firms had to check with headquarters in the home country and had a rigid return on investment to account for each year in the early years. This meant that when the decision on terms came from the United States headquarters after two or three months, the local Japanese firms had already obtained the contract.

NEED FOR SYSTEMATIC PLANNING AND CO-ORDINATION

Having emphasised the need for flexibility, it is, however, important to have a systematic approach to the planning and co-ordination of export activities. Despite the diversity in export markets, there is the possibility of transferring some of the learning as a result of previous mistakes and successes in exporting. In this respect it may be possible to cluster markets in the same economic region or trade bloc. In the systematic planning process, the following questions might be asked.

(a) How many export markets can be handled at once in production capability or management terms? (Two or three are recommended for smaller firms starting in exporting.)

(b) Will our strategy be to penetrate deeply two or three, or obtain a modest market share in six or eight, i.e. a depth or breadth approach to international marketing?

(c) Which markets are most feasible as a priority? Factors to consider include proximity, product fit, best contacts/agents, and cultural similarities.

(d) What will be the order for developing various international markets over the next five years?

On the co-ordination challenge, there will need to be maximum flexibility, while ensuring minimum duplication in management, documentation and transportation, where shared container systems and charter facilities are widely used. There should be one management co-ordinator for all international marketing activities with delegated authority to internal market managers or external agencies, or both. Co-ordination challenges include optimal distribution and other systems for the *market/product matrix* (*see* Fig. 39). Products (a), (b) and (c) might, for example,

	Markets			
	1	2	3	4
Products: (a)	Type adaptation Price Volume Network			
(b)				
(c)				

Fig. 39. *Market/product matrix.*

be three models of motor cars in a range. Each might need adaptation in the four distinct export markets in terms of type adaptation, pricing, volume and network most appropriate to that particular market. Some standard elements might be feasible in more than one market, and obviously some learning is transferable and transportation rationalisation possible across and between markets, depending on location and proximity one to the other.

Co-ordination will ensure feedback on market changes and their impact on other markets, if any. The terms "planning and co-ordination" may sometimes infer a passive rather than a dynamic interactive approach. However, in international marketing it is important that these terms are interpreted as dynamically innovative and creative to cope with environmental changes and vigorous competition.

MANAGING THE INTERNATIONAL MARKET PORTFOLIO

The challenge in international marketing is to:

(*a*) ensure that the firm has the optimum type and number of markets relevant to its production and management capability; and

(*b*) manage the portfolio in the most effective and efficient manner, thus ensuring that the firm is getting as much as possible out of each market and with the least resources possible.

The Boston Consulting Group approach was mentioned in Chapter 13. This is a useful model for displaying the total picture of international markets on a scale relative to their growth potential and market penetration/market share (*see* Fig. 27). However, it perhaps lacks the ability to project the dynamic which is so necessary in managing international market operations.

Key decisions arise with the analysis of potential markets clustered on the edge of the high growth, low market share section of the model. These markets need to be put in priority order for possible movement into the portfolio in the "problem children" section. Criteria will include potential growth in the given market for the specific product and the potential market penetration by the firm. Another decision at the margin will be the "dogs" in the portfolio, those with low market growth and minimal market penetration. If either feature shows little prospect of change or being changed, then the decision may have to be made to withdraw from the particular market(s).

The internal management challenges include moving the "problem children" markets into star position by greater penetration and stronger market share, and ensuring that maximum cash is provided by the "cash cows" for optimal use in promotion of the "problem children".

Despite the need for flexibility there is also a requirement for *control* because of the high costs of operating in a range of international markets. There are several potential problem areas which a well-devised control system might minimise, if not remove:

(*a*) lack of financial control overseas;
(*b*) duplication of sales offices;
(*c*) duplication of administration;
(*d*) conflicts over markets/geographic areas overseas; and
(*e*) failure of foreign operations to perform or report to expectations.

One approach to devising a control system might be as shown in Fig. 40.

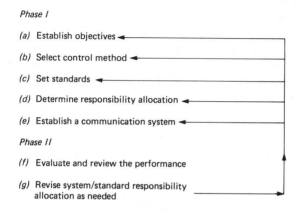

Phase I

(a) Establish objectives

(b) Select control method

(c) Set standards

(d) Determine responsibility allocation

(e) Establish a communication system

Phase II

(f) Evaluate and review the performance

(g) Revise system/standard responsibility
     allocation as needed

Fig. 40. *Devising a control system.*

All aspects of the policy will need to be reviewed and some revised after
Phase I, whether this is six months or one year. It is important to be precise
in specification of objectives, control and standards. In allocating
responsibility, ensure there is the capability and the resources to undertake
the task. Communications is a key area in international marketing. Language and cultural differences can limit the effectiveness of the technological progress of telex and global telephone networks in this important
area.

REVIEW AND RENEWAL OF PRIORITIES

It is most important to review and renew export market priorities on a
regular basis. In the 1950s and 1960s, it might have been tempting to advise
such a review every five years. However, in the 1980s, many firms review
their position every year, because of the very rapid rate of economic,
technical and political change. In some cases, because of inflation, currency changes and competition, firms continually review their situation.
Nigeria is a good example in recent times, where the scale of development
and importing policy have been affected by a reduction in funds available
from oil, and political upheavals. The intervention of governments and
changes in the regulations of trade blocs such as the EEC also demand
review of both the strategy and tactics of international marketing
operations. The successful international marketer needs to be a constant

innovator with a creative mind ready, willing and able to *anticipate*, rather than react to environmental changes.

SUMMARY

In this chapter, the need for flexibility has been stressed in all the planning for and co-ordination of international marketing operations. The two key areas of management are:

(*a*) the major decision regarding which markets to select in what priority, and which to reject in the appropriate order; and

(*b*) the management of the optimal mix of the existing international markets in the portfolio, involving a flexibility and versatility to export market penetration.

Finally, it is vital to design effective control systems. Regular review of *which* markets the firm selects, and *how* they are to be managed, is essential for successful international marketing planning and co-ordination.

QUESTIONS

1. As a potential export manager for British Leyland, suggest a systematic approach to planning a control system for their international marketing operations. (Note: this will involve obtaining and studying their annual report and accounts.)

2. A medium-sized Indian firm is considering developing its third and fourth export market in Germany and France, in addition to the United Kingdom and Denmark. Advise the firm on why a control system might help in co-ordinating these export market operations.

CHAPTER NINETEEN

Facilitating and Regulatory Agencies

OBJECTIVES

This chapter describes the role of facilitating and regulatory agencies at national and local level with special reference to the United Kingdom and Ireland.

A SUPPORTIVE ENVIRONMENT

Although the main thrust and inspiration for international marketing must come from the innovative and creative business owner and business leader, it is important that there is a supportive climate and "soil" for the export "acorns" to become established "oaks" in international markets. This climate should be politically stable and economically positive with quality products and services at reasonable competitive prices. One of the most positive environments in terms of national attitudes was a country in South-East Asia where the successful exporters were applauded as national heroes, with full public acclaim daily in both press and television.

In some developing countries, government facilitating agencies are more regulatory in operation, creating massive documentary barriers to their exporting private-sector colleagues. In one instance, between fifty and sixty documents needed to be completed before the products left the home market. However, in most countries, an effort is now being made to rationalise procedures and assist, through a range of agencies, the exporting community. In some instances, the government itself becomes an active partner in the export expansion plan.

ROLE OF FACILITATING AND REGULATORY AGENCIES

Most governments need to have full information on the products and services moving both ways across their frontiers. This information is required to monitor international trading performance, and to assess the impact on the balance of trade and balance of payments.

In addition, governments, in certain instances, may wish to monitor and control the movement of products. For instance, where there is a limited supply in the home country, or where there is a particular shortage of foreign currency or pressure on the domestic currency, imports may have to be curtailed. Examples of control imposed for political reasons include the embargo on trading with South Africa by some countries, and the limitation in allowing new high technology to the Soviet Union by the United States.

The major effort, however, goes into providing facilitating agencies to promote and assist exports in order to earn more foreign currency and create wealth for the home population. The roles of such agencies include the provision of information, promotional work, and sometimes financial aid and insurance. There is usually one main agency in most exporting countries, industrialised and developing, which is in fact often called an export promotion agency or board, under the aegis of a department of government such as the Ministry of Commerce, Industry or Trade. While some reference was made to developing countries in earlier chapters, it is proposed now to discuss in more detail the cases of the United Kingdom and Ireland.

THE UNITED KINGDOM

British Overseas Trade Board

The main facilitating body is the British Overseas Trade Board, which was set up in January 1972 to help British exporters. Its members are drawn from government and industry, the President being the Secretary of State for Trade and Industry, and the Chairman a leading industrialist.

The Board provides information, advice and help to the exporter. It does this by directing, through divisions of the Department of Trade and Industry, the gathering, storing and dissemination of overseas market information, and by the provision of advice and help to individual firms, by the organisation of collective trade promotions, and by the stimulation of export promotion activity.

The Export Marketing Research Scheme of the BOTB is designed to help and encourage United Kingdom firms to undertake marketing research overseas as an essential part of their export effort. It does this by providing a free professional overseas marketing research advisory service, and financial support for export marketing research (up to 50 per cent of the total cost).

The Export Data Branch of the BOTB includes the Overseas Tariffs and Regulations (OTAR) section. This can supply information about tariffs and non-tariff barriers which British exports may have to face. Subjects covered range from customs laws and duties to weights and measures regulations. Its work is complementary to the Simplification of International Trade Procedures Board (SITPRO) and Technical Help to Exporters (THE) in this field (*see* below). It notably provides information about overseas agency legislation.

The Export Data Branch also provides the Export Intelligence Service (EIS). This is a computerised information service, which daily distributes export intelligence to subscribers. This includes overseas enquiries for products or services, calls for tender, details of agents seeking United

Kingdom principals, early notification of projects overseas and many other items offering new trade opportunities.

The Overseas Status Report Service enables British exporters who already know of likely potential overseas representatives for their products or services to obtain current and individual assessments of them. Such a report gives, for example, particulars of the standing of a company; the scope of its activities; and its ability to cover the territory in which it claims to operate, if an agent or distributor. These status reports are not credit ratings, and the latter type of information is best sought through a bank or commercial enquiry agency.

The Market Entry Guarantee Scheme (MEGS) aims to help smaller and medium-sized firms to break into new overseas markets, or to mount a new initiative designed to capture a significantly increased amount of business in an existing overseas market, and to share in the risks involved. The scheme funds half of certain overhead costs associated with a new venture. In return, the department makes a flat-rate charge of 3 per cent of its funding, and in addition takes a levy on sales receipts. If the venture is unsuccessful, after a period of time the firm is relieved of any shortfall in repayment that remains due.

The Fairs and Promotions Branch of the BOTB operates through a number of schemes to encourage firms to participate in overseas trade fairs with a view to increasing exports of British-made goods and services. In the joint venture scheme, a number of firms in an industry take part, with BOTB support, in a collective presentation of United Kingdom goods or services at a specialised trade fair overseas under the sponsorship of an approved trade association or chamber of commerce. In the British Pavilion scheme, provided enough firms wish to participate, the BOTB organises British pavilions at certain international trade fairs which are organised in national sections.

The Market Advisory Service provides information about the prospects for selling particular goods or services in overseas markets, advice about how to exploit the opportunities those markets offer, and, where appropriate, advice about how best to secure effective local representation. An exporter wishing to use the service discusses his choice of market with the BOTB and completes a questionnaire which is sent to the commercial department of the British Embassy, High Commission or Consulate-General in the country concerned. The commercial department report will cover such aspects as local demand, the strengths and patterns of competition from locally produced and/or imported goods, etc.

There are several further divisions to the BOTB, but an exhaustive list would not contribute much to the already apparent breadth of services described.

Department of Trade and Industry
The DTI also contributes in its own right to export marketing. Two notable

organs are the Exports to Europe Branch, and the Exports to Japan Unit (EJU). The former provides a single focus for the co-ordination of trade promotion in Western Europe, and the stimulation of exports in selected product sectors where there are particular opportunities; and a single point of enquiry for all country-based information about the various markets of Western Europe. The EJU provides an advisory service in conjunction with overseas appointments, the Foreign and Commonwealth Office, and the BOTB's Japan Trade Advisory Group on all aspects of exporting to Japan. It can also put the exporter in touch with the range of services available from the BOTB.

Statistics and Market Intelligence Library (SMIL)
This is provided by the government for public use. A great deal of information on overseas markets is available here. This includes directories, development plans, and apposite United Kingdom and overseas trade statistics.

Simplification of International Trade Procedures Board (SITPRO)
This was established in 1970 to "guide, stimulate and assist the rationalisation of international trade procedures, and the documentation and information flow associated with them". It operates on an annual grant from the BOTB and acts independently of the government, within its agreed terms of reference. Board membership is drawn from a wide range of commercial and official interests, including carriers, freight forwarders, bankers and HM customs.

Technical Help to Exporters (THE)
This is part of the British Standards Institution and is a non-profit making organisation. It currently receives a government grant to help finance its services to British industry, which are designed to assist with technical exporting problems.

Export Credits Guarantee Department (ECGD)
This is a government department responsible to the Secretary of State for Trade and Industry (*see also* Chapter 14). It was established in 1919 and is the world's oldest and most experienced export credit insurance organisation. The ECGD's primary function is to encourage British exports of goods and services by giving guarantees. It also insures new investment overseas. The ECGD can help the exporter by providing insurance against the risk of not being paid by overseas customers. This covers default, insolvency, exchange difficulties or import restrictions. It can also help by providing guarantees to banks under which companies may obtain finance for their export credit transactions, often at favourable rates of interest. The ECGD can provide insurance for new investment

overseas against the main "political" or non-commercial risks such as war, expropriation and restriction on remittances.

Non-official organisations
In addition, there is in the United Kingdom, and publicised by the BOTB, a wide range of related and non-official trade organisations:

(*a*) British Invisible Exporters Council;
(*b*) Nationalised Industrial Overseas Group (NIOG);
(*c*) export clubs (*see* below).

There are also several area advisory groups, as listed below:
Australia and New Zealand Trade Advisory Committee
Trade Group for Israel
British and South East Asian Trade Association
Committee for Middle East Trade
East European Trade Council
European Trade Committee
Hong Kong Trade Advisory Group
Japan Trade Advisory Group
Korea Trade Advisory Group
Latin America Trade Advisory Group
North America Trade Advisory Group
Sino-British Trade Council
Tropical Africa Advisory Group
United Kingdom/South Africa Trade Association
West Indies Trade Advisory Group

IRELAND

Brief details were given of the Irish Export Board (*Córas Tráchtála*, or CTT) in Chapter 4. This Board is probably more proactive than the British Overseas Trade Board, which tends to be reactive. It also has a very dynamic network of overseas offices operating on a commercial philosophy, rather than a "diplomatic service" style *modus operandi*. This network is in addition to Irish Embassy offices, but works closely with diplomatic staff. The network includes in the UK: London, Manchester, Birmingham, Bristol and Glasgow; in Europe: Brussels, Amsterdam, Copenhagen, Dusseldorf, Paris, Milan, Stockholm, Zurich, Madrid, Vienna and Moscow; and in the rest of the world: Chicago, Toronto, Sydney, Tokyo, the Middle East, Nigeria, Singapore and the People's Republic of China.

The Irish Export Board played a leading role in broadening the product base and the market base of Irish exports during the period 1962–82. A mainly agricultural-based economy now has, with the help of the Industrial Development Authority (IDA), a wide and diverse portfolio of industries.

It has also (with CTT guidance) diversified its international market portfolio, reducing its dependence on the United Kingdom market from nearly 70 per cent to 38.8 per cent over a twenty-year period. The massive expansion of Irish exports from IR£647 million in 1972 to IR£5,688 million in 1982 is testimony to the leadership role played by this dynamic board. It is a tribute to this board that many developing countries send their government officials and export leaders to study the Irish Export Promotion model and methodology and request CTT senior officials to visit them and advise on the formation and development of export development agencies for Third World countries.

ADAPTATION OF BRITISH AND IRISH METHODS TO DEVELOPING NATIONS

Care must be taken when considering the adoption of one export development method by another country, particularly a developing country. Many factors must be considered:

(a) different tradition and political system;

(b) different international trade setting (EEC and Europe as compared to other Asian, African and Latin American trade blocs);

(c) often greater government participation in both production and exporting through state production services and state trading corporations in some Third World countries;

(d) distinct differences in climate and stage of agricultural and industrial development, giving different product profile;

(e) possibly less-developed transport and communications networks, both internal and external, in Third World countries;

(f) in terms of manpower, often less training facilities and lower salary scales which inhibit the ability of a Third World government agency to recruit the appropriate management and export advisory staff from the private sector.

However, having taken into account this wide range of internal and external factors, there is still much to be learnt by developing countries from European methods, such as those used by Ireland's CTT.

EXPORT CLUBS

Exporting initiatives in various countries can receive an important impetus from a network of national and local export clubs. These clubs can share vital market, production adaptation, pricing and distribution information and encouragement with their members. The better clubs are always self-help groups, although recognised, encouraged and publicised by national government export promotion agencies. Export clubs usually meet monthly and can have a market focus such as "a Middle East Exporters

Club" or an industry focus such as "a Craft and Giftware Exporters Club". The British Overseas Trade Board Annual Report, 1983, lists forty-one export clubs, organised on a local and regional basis.

EDUCATIONAL INSTITUTIONS

Institutions of education can play a vital local and national role in supporting exporters and potential exporters. College and university services to the national export effort can include the following:

(a) information centres on international markets, and international trade, across a range of relevant industries;
(b) consultancy and advisory services by lecturers with practical experience of training and education in international marketing;
(c) undergraduate and postgraduate education and training in international marketing, with relevant locally sponsored export projects.

An example of (c) at the University of Ulster in Northern Ireland has been the provision of consultancy teams of mature students (aged 25–35 years) with five years' marketing experience, to investigate the Irish market and the Dutch market for existing and potential Northern Ireland exporting firms. These have been financed two-thirds by government, one-third by the company for field work, and a modest contribution by the consulting students for general administration. All assignments included preliminary desk research and production capability investigation, followed by field work in the export target market based in Dublin and Amsterdam. The assignments were part of the two-year part-time postgraduate Diploma in Marketing (International Marketing area).

SCOPE FOR INTER-INSTITUTIONAL CO-OPERATION

It is important that all organisations supporting the national export effort are mobilised and co-ordinated, while having their own identity and task, as it is easy for the support system to be fragmented and lacking in overall synergy. This is especially true in developing countries where expertise is scarce and dissipated within different organisations. A good example of inter-institutional co-operation has been seen in the 1980s in Thailand, where a National Export Marketing Training Centre was developed by harnessing the co-operation and skills of three agencies: government, the universities and the private sector. The planning and operation of this vital National Training Centre involves the following partners: export trainers from the Ministry of Commerce Export Service Centre, three universities around Bangkok, and private sector export club members with live case studies to be used in the national training effort. Already tripartite teams from the three agencies have developed an Export Marketing Case Book for Thailand.

SUMMARY

In this chapter, a local and national climate positive to exporting has been highlighted as an important factor in national export performance. Supportive agencies in the UK and Ireland have been described. Such Western European examples are often used as models by export development agencies in the Third World. Other support systems include local exporters clubs and educational institutions.

QUESTIONS

1. As a potential export marketing advisor to Kenya, advise on the setting up of an Export Development Agency, contrasting your model with the BOTB.

2. Outline what local potential there is in your country for greater use of the educational facilities and export clubs in assisting exporters.

CHAPTER TWENTY

The Multinationals and International Marketing

OBJECTIVES

No book on international marketing would be complete without a section on the multinationals. This chapter examines the development and key role of multinational companies in international marketing.

DEFINITIONS

There are many definitions of a multinational company. Raymond Vernon says: "the term 'multinational enterprise' is sometimes confusing and always imprecise; but what I have in mind here is simply a cluster of corporations of diverse nationalities joined together by ties of common ownership and responsive to a common management strategy.' Another definition is offered by Jack N. Behrman: "The essence of the multi-national enterprise is that it is attempting to treat the various national markets as though they were one—to the extent permitted by governments at least." The modern multinational is noted for treating the world as its market-place and production site. There are many examples of these, with production plants in various countries and continents, and international marketing organised on a divisional headquarters basis, such as a European or United States division. Many of these modern multinationals are multi-million-pound operations, often larger than some nation states, and collectively they handle a very high proportion of international trade. It was this size and power which caused some resentment in the 1960s and 1970s, as these industrial giants attempted to minimise the impact of world recession, and take advantage of recession lag-time in various parts of the world.

MOTIVES AND STAGES IN MULTINATIONAL DEVELOPMENT

Multinationals develop from various rationales and origins. The United States, Europe and Japan have proved to be the sources of the majority of today's multinationals. The following are some reasons offered for investing abroad.

(*a*) To overcome tariff and import barriers and regulations. The formation of the EEC attracted many direct investments in the 1960s and 1970s.

(*b*) To obtain or use local raw materials. This could be part of the case for investment in some developing countries.

(*c*) To reduce or eliminate high transportation costs, such as trans-Atlantic, trans-Pacific and Europe/Far East costs.

(*d*) To obtain incentives offered by host governments. An example of this is the successful marketing efforts world-wide of the Irish Industrial Development Authority packages.

(*e*) To obtain and maintain market positions. This could be part of the strategy for European investment in the United States, and vice versa.

(*f*) To control quality in the manufacture of specialised items such as health care products.

(*g*) To follow and effectively compete with a rival firm.

Of course there are many more reasons and combinations of the above, and other reasons which apply to particular firms. In many cases, it is simply a natural form of evolution, one of a series of stages of development of an enterprise, as outlined below.

Stage 1: exporting through home-based export markets or domestic agents.

Stage 2: export department formed to sell directly to overseas importer/buyer.

Stage 3: overseas agents appointed in foreign market.

Stage 4: sales branch or office established abroad for promotional and sales work.

Stage 5: sales subsidiary firm established and domiciled in the foreign market.

Stage 6: manufacturing and production facility established in the foreign market.

Stage 7: overseas operations integrated, with either headquarters or divisional headquarters making the key management decisions.

However, the keen competition in recent years for mobile investment has meant that many firms move to stage 6, without going through the gradual evolution outlined above.

MULTINATIONAL COMPANY AND HOST GOVERNMENT RELATIONSHIP

During the 1960s and 1970s, there appeared to be an anti-multinational lobby in many host countries, particularly in some developing countries. The power and size of multinationals was feared and in many cases national governments drew up strict regulations to protect national interests. One example of these rules included the insistence on majority shareholding being locally owned. India was one country which was willing to allow Coca-Cola to withdraw, rather than allow the breaking of this rule.

As a result of possible alienation and adverse publicity, some multinationals produced very impressive booklets on their particular contribution to the host nation's work. This approach was used by Lever Brothers in Sri Lanka with some success.

Winning a reputation for good corporate citizenship of the host country was a high priority for many multinationals in the 1970s. The guiding principles laid down by the Canadian government Foreign Investment Review Agency are interesting to note. They included the following.

(*a*) Pursue a high degree of autonomy in the exercise of decision-making and risk-taking functions.

(*b*) Develop as an integral part of the Canadian operation an autonomous capability for technological innovation, and for production, marketing, purchasing and accounting.

(*c*) Retain in Canada a sufficient share of earnings to give strong financial support to the growth and entrepreneurial potential of the Canadian operation, having in mind a fair return to shareholders on capital invested.

(*d*) Strive for a full international mandate for innovation and market development, when it will enable the Canadian company to improve its efficiency by specialisation of production operations.

(*e*) Aggressively pursue and develop market opportunities throughout international markets, as well as Canada.

(*f*) Extend the processing in Canada of natural resource products to the maximum extent feasible on an economic basis.

(*g*) Search out and develop economic sources of supply in Canada for domestically produced goods and for professional and other services.

(*h*) Foster a "Canadian outlook" within management, as well as enlarged career opportunities within Canada, by promoting Canadians to senior and middle management positions, and by including a majority of Canadians on boards of directors of all Canadian companies.

(*i*) Create a financial structure that provides opportunity for substantial equity participation in the Canadian enterprise by the Canadian public.

(*j*) Pursue a pricing policy designed to assure a fair and reasonable return to the company and to Canada for all goods and services sold abroad, including sales to parent companies and other affiliates.

(*k*) Regularly publish information on the operations and financial position of the firm.

(*l*) Give appropriate support to recognised national objectives and established government programmes, while resisting any direct or indirect pressure from foreign governments or associated companies to act in a contrary manner.

(*m*) Participate in Canadian social and cultural life and support those institutions that are concerned with the intellectual, social and cultural advancement of the Canadian community.

Several host countries in Europe have many of these principles in mind now when seeking to attract mobile investment. Host countries are particularly keen on having more than just a production facility. There is an increasing effort being made to attract the full range of R & D and marketing functions to ensure new business development and more autonomy for the subsidiary firm.

MULTINATIONAL SUBSIDIARY AND HEADQUARTERS RELATIONSHIP

There is obviously scope for some tension between the subsidiary and headquarters in terms of controlling the development and economic destiny of the overseas unit, and the two sets of possible external constraints/regulations—that of the host government and the domestic government.

The overall framework, including the relationships, are shown in Fig. 41. Subsidiaries B and C may have domestic markets to serve as well as

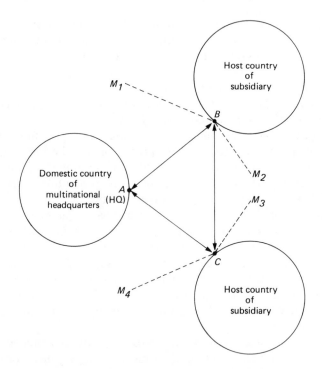

Fig. 41. *Headquarters/subsidiary relationships.*

many other markets in various countries (M_1–M_4). As mentioned earlier, areas of contention are research and development and marketing departments. When a multinational may have up to eight production centres in five different host nation states, serving perhaps twelve different markets (including those five host countries), one begins to imagine the complexity of decisions as to which production centre serves which markets, and with which range of products (from a portfolio of possibly twenty products). There is, of course, scope for tension not only between head office and subsidiary, but also between one subsidiary and another.

CHALLENGE FOR INTERNATIONAL MARKETERS

From earlier parts of this chapter, it may be seen that there is the challenge of complexity and uncertainty in the international marketing of multi-nationals. Much emphasis is placed on reducing the area of uncertainty by effective up-to-date market information and management training. There is scope for a staged development plan in sales, marketing including market research, product planning, and management. It is also possible to specialise through the sheer size of the marketing function. One of the often less-publicised benefits of locating the marketing function in a host country is the marketing training provided for local staff who may be recruited later by indigenous firms.

One of the best training experiences for international marketers is the movement to various locations in a multinational group, adapting to various cultures and observing various market penetration tactics at first hand.

SUMMARY

Multinationals have the experience of years of cultural adaptation, both in staff management and adaptation in product and market management. They have to contend with various political and economic influences in many different languages. Complexity and uncertainty is their weekly diet, and for all of these reasons, placement in various marketing functions across a range of locations is one of the best and most professional training experiences for international marketing.

QUESTIONS

1. Discuss a possible rationale for the increasing Japanese investment in Europe.

2. As a representative of a multinational, outline the possible advantages to a developing country of your firm being allowed to set up a subsidiary company locally.

CHAPTER TWENTY-ONE

Future Trends in International Marketing

OBJECTIVES

Not much is certain in the world of today, but there are few who doubt the continued growth in international trade. This chapter outlines some possible future changes in trading patterns, and aims to encourage the reader to explore how such changes will impact on international marketing.

GROWTH IN INTERNATIONAL TRADE

It is clear that the world will continue to grow more interdependent in trading terms. There are even signs that some of the industrialised nations (20 per cent of the world's population) will see the good long-term self-interest of ensuring that some of the underdeveloped 80 per cent of the population have the means to improve their condition with greater purchasing power. This increasing North–South trade—as urged in the Brandt report—will be accompanied by South–South inter-trading between developing countries at various stages of the development curve. The emergence of trade blocs such as the Association of South-East Asian Nations (ASEAN) will accelerate this inter-trading. Similarly, in the industrialised world, the further development of the European Economic Community (EEC) and other North–North inter-trading relationships will mean greater international trading, with island economies such as Ireland pushing for ever-escalating export targets. In the latter case, this might be from IR£8.5 billion in 1984 to perhaps IR£20–25 billion by the turn of the century.

SHIFTING INTERNATIONAL TRADING "HIGHWAYS" AND RELATIONSHIPS

There is now the obvious prospect of Japan and the Far East countries becoming growth leaders in industrial development and international trade, directly and through their international network of companies and subsidiaries. As this world industrial leadership moves from the United States to the Far East the main trading "highway" which represents the "taking of the baton" by Japan is the Pacific. This is just as the Atlantic was the main trading "highway" when the United States took the leadership baton from Britain over the last hundred years. Emergence of the Pacific "highway" could mean a shift in industrial and economic power to the

United States West Coast, rather than the United States East Coast, where it has resided in the past decades of this century.

The United States and Japan together have more than a 35 per cent share of world trade in manufactured products, according to the British Overseas Trade Board Annual Report 1982. This could rise to over 40 per cent by the turn of the century, as both countries *increased* their share by nearly 6 per cent in the past ten years, Japan contributing 4.2 per cent of this. West Germany and the United Kingdom in contrast have *reduced* their combined share by 2.2 per cent in the same period (although West Germany remains the one exceptionally strong country in Europe in world trade in manufacturing).

Certain factors can distort the world "highway" concept. These include growth in South–South trade, increasing Japanese exports to South East Asian countries and Europe, the increasing interest in EEC countries' export performance, and the economics of air transport with increasing volumes of international trade going by air. Some of these will be discussed later. Additional examples include Brazil's trade with other Latin American countries, and with former Portuguese colonies in Africa.

There would appear to be scope for increased use of barter in international trading relationships. This is explained by some as resulting from a failure in international financing arrangements, shortages in foreign currencies in various countries, particularly developing countries, and rampant inflation and near bankruptcies in other countries. There is growing evidence of this barter phenomenon in East–West trading, with restrictions by some Western countries on high technology transfer. In trade between the industrialised and developing nations, it has enabled some importing by developing countries where there is a dire shortage of foreign currencies. For similar reasons, barter might also be a feasible way forward for South–South trading, and self-help in various trade blocs.

EXPORTING OPPORTUNITIES FOR VARIOUS COUNTRIES

For the Third World, as mentioned earlier, local developing countries could be emerging as possible export markets. The beginnings of this may be seen in South East Asia, where additionally Japan, Australia and the Middle East are potential international marketing targets. To African countries, South Africa and the Middle East are potential target markets, if politics will allow relationships to develop. In the Latin American countries once again local markets are emerging, particularly Mexico and Brazil and of course the United States. Provided the quality and finish is right, together with packaging and presentation, all markets in Europe and North America will be increasingly possible international marketing targets for developing countries, particularly in textiles and craft and giftware industries.

In the United States the rapid development of free trade zones has tended to give an increasing focus to international marketing, which seemed to be neglected because of the large home market. Canada, Latin America, Europe and the Far East will be possible targets both for direct exporting and overseas investment location.

The Japanese success in international marketing has been admired and perhaps envied by most of the world's international marketing community. They are likely to continue their "cascade" approach described earlier—putting purchasing power in the hands of local neighbouring countries in the Far East. They will continue to build up their international trading network, perhaps with an even greater investment in overseas subsidiaries to de-emphasise their direct exporting penetration performances. Their approach to the industrialisation of their neighbour China will be interesting to observe.

China, as many observers have already noted, appears to be developing rapidly as an industrial power with reportedly large underdeveloped reserves of natural resources (and approximately one-quarter of the world's population). There are many signs that the Chinese are selecting the best of the Western world's approaches to industrial development and are quickly establishing links with Western countries and trade blocs. One recent example of such a link was the signing by the EEC of a five-year contract to develop China's first business school, training the faculty and developing a special industry-related full-time programme for Masters in Business Administration, with subjects such as marketing and international marketing. The dedication of the people of this culture would suggest that by the turn of the century they will be supplying not just Asian markets but also European and United States markets.

In the United Kingdom there continues to be a strong emphasis on international marketing. There is now an attempt to provide a special physical focus for international marketing, through the designation in early 1984 of six freeports—three at international airports and three at sea-ports. The big challenge will be the further development of visible exports, especially to Europe, in the period 1973–1983 exports to the EEC increased from 32.6 per cent to 43.9 per cent. The United States, Middle East and the developing countries of South East Asia and Latin America must also be possible international marketing targets. Once again China could well emerge as an impressive target market by the year 2000.

The Soviet Union continues to look to other centrally planned economies but the nations of the EEC, Middle East and South East Asia could prove to be possible market targets. The markets of African countries and China are more difficult to predict.

DEVELOPMENTS IN MECHANISMS AND FACILITATING AGENCIES

There is little doubt that satellite television and multi-channel television will revolutionise the international market-place, possibly leading to more standardisation and world products of the Coca-Cola and McDonald's type. This technological development could also accelerate the growing interest in multi-language facilities by the international marketing and business communities generally. With the growth of international business and international media, more and more "world citizens" will emerge who will feel at home in many cultures and trading centres, and be less dependent on any one culture or nation.

Another phenomenon of the last quarter of the twentieth century is the widespread development of freeports or free trade zones. This can be seen in the United States, Latin America, Asia and Africa, as well as in Europe. It is forecast that over 20 per cent of world trade will be handled through this world-wide network by the 1990s. It will be interesting to see if these emerge as the main national and international focal points not just for international trading, but for industrial development. There are early signs of this in developing countries, where in one case in Asia over 100,000 people are employed in manufacturing and processing. An early European model on these lines was the Shannon Airport free trade zone in Ireland, where a new town developed later alongside the airport.

A possible future development might be the emergence of consortia of freeports across different continents. This could mean that a European freeport could link with an Asian freeport and one or two American free trade zones, referring clients one to the other, in the same way as hotel chains become associated world-wide.

At the micro level of the firm, it is possible that more and more smaller firms employing as few as twenty or thirty people might become interested in international marketing. Through attending the growing number of exporters clubs (*see* Chapter 19), they might become interested in particular markets and meet other colleagues owning firms producing complementary products. This could lead to increasing numbers of *group export marketing projects*, where four or five firms with complementary products forming a coherent product cluster set up export market investigations and later marketing and sales/distribution centres on a shared basis, each contributing 20 or 25 per cent of the expenses. This trend could be facilitated by the existence of freeport networks with streamlined documentation facilities and customs duty-free advantages. Such group export marketing is already a reality in developing, as well as industrialised, countries. In addition to reducing the cost per firm of export market entry, there is the potential for the sharing of larger orders from multinational companies.

It is possible that as government interest in national export performance grows, a more active role will be taken by governments in international marketing, either by setting up international trading state companies or by seeking to become partners with the private sector in international market developments. Many observers have commented on the close relationship and teamwork between the Japanese government, their banks and private sector exporters.

A key role will continue to be played by the International Trade Centre in Geneva (*see* Chapter 4). This Centre, through its impressive training office and many world-wide projects, is already making a major contribution to the expansion of developing countries' exports around the world. The increasing emphasis on helping developing countries to help themselves through improved infrastructure and institutional capability for export development is likely to make a major contribution to Third World export performance.

SUMMARY

In this chapter, possible future trends in international trade have been discussed, together with a range of factors which can impact on international marketing by the turn of the century. Just as in the past, the future looks full of surprises for the international marketer—many, many more than in domestic marketing. This is what makes the whole activity so exciting and rewarding—overcoming the unexpected and the unknown.

The accuracy of predictions and validity of scenarios is not what is important. If this chapter stimulates the reader to question further and anticipate what the future holds, providing for the unexpected, then it will have met its objectives. This is what is meant by facing with energy, creativity and enthusiasm the challenges and approaches of international marketing.

QUESTIONS

1. As a United Kingdom exporter of micro software, discuss the challenges and approaches you face in the next ten years.

2. As a potential export manager in a Thai silk international trading company, discuss the scope and challenges facing your company by the year 2000.

APPENDIX I

Export Promotion
in Thailand

NOTE: The following extracts are taken from *Thailand's Exporters 1980–1981*, published by the Thailand Ministry of Commerce.

Exporting is an important activity for developing countries, earning much needed foreign currency and improving the standard of living of the populace by creating employment. The governments of all developing countries, therefore, implement whatever measures they consider expedient to accelerate the growth of exports.

That Thailand adopts an aggressive approach to export promotion can be seen by the target figure of 136,000 million baht set for 1980, an increase of 25.46 per cent on 1979. And an even greater increase is planned for 1981.

In order to meet the above target, the government has stipulated a number of financial, commercial and investment measures to render facilities to investors, manufacturers and exporters in placing their products in foreign markets.

As a monetary incentive, exporters are granted tax compensation and tariff reimbursement on exported goods. On the investment side, privileges are given to investors who will produce export goods specially for local trading companies.

From the commercial aspect, the Ministry of Commerce has implemented a number of measures to render more facilities and increase export efficiency, as follows.

1. *The Export Development Committee.* The Ministry of Commerce has established the Export Development Committee, which is chaired by the Minister of Commerce and membered by the under secretaries of other ministries concerned with manufacture and export, with a mandate to guide export planning and remove problems and barriers.

2. *Trade Missions.* In order to expand both the spread and penetration of the overseas markets, the Ministry of Commerce has encouraged the private sector to undertake a number of trade missions to the EEC and other European countries, Australia, the Middle East, Japan, the USA and others.

3. *Export Promotion Organisation.* Several departments are involved in this work.

3.1. *The Office of the Commercial Counsellor.* This office, under the office of the Under Secretary of State, operates offices in 24 countries (to be increased to 29 in 1981), dealing with policy formation and negotiations on trade problems at government level.

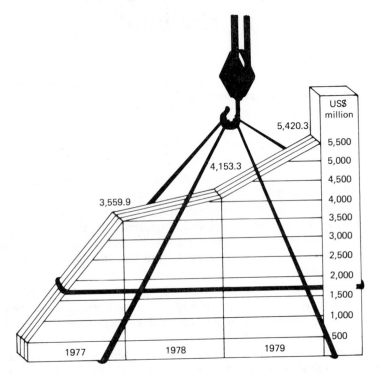

USS million

5,500
5,000
4,500
4,000
3,500
3,000
2,500
2,000
1,500
1,000
500

5,420.3
4,153.3
3,559.9

1977   1978   1979

Source: *Thailand's Exporters—1980–1981*, Ministry of Commerce, Thailand.

Fig. 42. *The climbing exports of Thailand.*

3.2. *The Department of Foreign Trade.* Also participates in trade negotiations relating to certain goods, mainly traditional exports, as well as taking responsibility for standardisation and export licences.

3.2.1. *The Establishment of Export Regulations.* To ensure maximum benefits to exporters, the number of exporters is controlled and quantities and minimum prices for each category of exportable goods are established.

3.2.2. *The Establishment of Quality Standards for Exportable Goods.* Quality standards ensure importers that the goods they receive will be up to the required standard.

3.3. *The Department of Business Economics.* Represents Thailand in tariff barrier negotiations and international trade agreements.

3.4. *The Department of Commercial Relations.* To further broaden export markets, the Ministry of Commerce has inaugurated the Department of Commercial Relations with the aim of promoting exports by means of providing services to exporters and foreign importers. To meet its objectives, The Department of Commercial Relations diversified its activities into:

3.4.1. *General Administration.* The Office of the Secretary of State is assigned to handle this activity. Its role is to take care of personnel management and budget allocation for the prompt success of the Department's objectives.

3.4.2. *Export Services—The Export Service Centre.* The Export Service Centre is assigned to provide advisory services, with a view to develop exports of domestically produced goods. The advisory services fit the needs of exporters, especially those seeking new markets for target products. The work of the Export Service Centre is carried out by the following sections:

3.4.2.1. *Trade Advisory Section.* This section provides general advisory information to exporters and helps solve export problems. The section also acts as co-ordinator between exporters and importers or foreign trade missions, which come to Thailand as potential buyers for local goods. Services include accumulating, analysing and researching market data, both by category and country.

With the dual purpose of (1) achieving quicker and wider expansion of Thai goods in foreign markets and (2) ensuring exporters of the latest market data from overseas, the Export Service Centre has established five Trade Centres in foreign countries, as follows:

1. New York Trade Centre	New York, USA
2. Frankfurt Trade Centre	Frankfurt, West Germany
3. Sydney Trade Centre	Sydney, Australia
4. Los Angeles Trade Centre	Los Angeles, USA
5. Vienna Trade Centre	Vienna, Austria
6. EEC-ASEAN	site under consideration

In the case of sufficient data not being locally available, the Export Service Centre can collect the relevant information from the Trade Centres and channel it speedily to the required destination. The following responsibilities are also carried out by the Trade Advisory Section:

A. *Promotion of Export Joint Marketing Groups.* It is the policy of the Department to encourage the grouping of exporters in order to improve production, strengthen bargaining power and eliminate internal competition. The policy aims at convincing exporters of the importance of grouping and creating a stronger feeling of unity among those who share mutual markets or products.

The underlying concept is that exporters should be organised in groups according to the category of their goods in order to find markets and win bigger orders for a higher profit. Manufacturers are gradually accepting this concept—to the benefit of all.

B. *Licensing.* The object of this policy is to encourage foreign manufacturers to license Thai producers to manufacture products for export under the trademark of the licensing company, and to find local manufacturers for foreign companies who will export products under its own trademark.

C. *Selling Missions*. Two or three selling missions are sent abroad annually to contribute to the work of exports. Some of the missions are sent to study the import structure of the countries visited, and evaluate at first hand the character and development of the market. The missions, which usually consist of businessmen accompanied by an adviser from the Department of Commercial Relations, have been sponsored by international organisations, such as the EEC. In addition, buying missions from abroad are welcomed by the arrangement of contacts and meetings with Thai manufacturers and exporters to facilitate direct purchasing. Factory visits and field trips are organised and follow-up procedure is monitored.

3.4.2.2. *Trade Information Services Section*. This section performs the function of collecting trade statistics of all nations world-wide, such as the movement and present state of overseas markets, information on rates of taxes and tariffs, import procedures, trade regulations and other market requirements for special products. To improve decision-making and business efficiency, exporters can acquire information on market needs and movements and can identify competitors. Under academic guidance from the International Trade Centre, Geneva, the Export Service Centre can provide exporters with up-to-date and internationally accepted trade data. At the Export Service Centre premises, microfilm data on international import statistics, covering 1,800 kinds of goods, is available to the public. In addition, there is a library of some 4,000 volumes and 343 periodicals in English and Thai.

3.4.2.3. *Seminar and Training Section*. This section is considered of great importance in furthering the work of the Centre. As some Thai businessmen still have limited experience in the field, the role of the section in training both businessmen and government officials is crucial.

The section arranges seminars to disseminate knowledge regarding market movements and government measures, both Thai and foreign, which affect businessmen and officials involved in exporting.

Training concentrates mainly on familiarisation with export marketing techniques while seminars aim to acquaint participants with market movements and ways of overcoming problems and barriers that affect the business of the private sector. Exporters and government officials are also sent overseas to attend seminars and training sessions, with the co-operation and assistance of several United Nations organisations and the EEC. In co-operation with the EEC, special programmes are also arranged to assist inter-ASEAN and ASEAN–EEC trade.

3.4.2.4. *Trade Centre Co-ordination Section*. This section co-operates closely with the Thai Trade Centres overseas in disseminating data on overseas markets compiled from reports made by the Thai Trade Centres, and returns data on local manufacturing for the benefit of importers in foreign countries.

3.4.2.5. *Product Adaptation Section*. This section has the responsibility of encouraging local manufacturers to produce products of internationally required standard. Potential products are selected for despatch, via the Trade Centre Co-Ordination Section, to Thai Trade Centres overseas, in order to test market reaction.

3.4.3. *Trade Promotion Division.* This division provides manufacturers and exporters with the service of promoting Thai goods both at home and abroad. In addition to taking part in international trade exhibitions in other countries, the section organises local trade fairs and undertakes surveys of products and raw materials.

The direct promotion of Thai goods through participation in international trade exhibitions has the following objectives:

(1) to widen the market for Thai goods in foreign countries;

(2) to increase exports in both quantity and value as a means to decreasing the trade deficit;

(3) to open opportunities for importers, wholesalers and retailers to make direct purchase agreements with Thai suppliers.

Since local trade fairs are important in terms of stimulating local traders and producers subsequently to participate in international trade exhibitions, the Department of Commercial Relations organises about twelve local trade fairs per year at the Trade Centre Exhibition Hall in Bangkok and about six per year in the provinces.

3.4.4. *Public Relations Activities for Export Promotion.* This function is carried out by the Trade Information Division. In addition to issuing numerous publications directly concerned with the state of production and other relevant data for overseas importers, this division disseminates news on foreign markets in order to guide local production to meet export objectives. The division publishes a variety of publications on all aspects of exporting, such as export data, market information, production and trends in overseas markets, for the benefit of Thai manufacturers and exporters, as well as overseas importers. The publications take the form of directories, leaflets, brochures and other specific printed matter for use in export campaigns.

The aim of the public relations activities is to familiarise exporters with government measures in promoting exports and acquaint them of incentives offered by the government sector. Public relations activities are carried out in close co-operation with the media—press, radio and television—in order to keep the public informed of export developments and activities.

Specially noteworthy publications of the division include—*Thailand's Exporters* and *Thailand Industrial Directory*—one of these bi-annual publications appearing each year. The division also publishes a quarterly—*Thailand Exporting*—and other occasional papers.

APPENDIX I

TRADE EXHIBITIONS TO BE ATTENDED BY THE
DEPARTMENT OF COMMERCIAL RELATIONS IN 1981

Venue	Date	Products
1. International Green Week, Berlin, W. Germany	Jan. 23–Feb. 1, 1981	Agricultural products and food
2. International Spring Fair, Birmingham, England	Feb. 1–5, 1981	Jewellery
3. International Nuremberg Toy Fair, Nuremberg, W. Germany	Feb. 5–11, 1981	Toys and games
4. Inhorgenta, Munich, W. Germany	Feb. 14–17, 1981	Jewellery
5. Frankfurt International Spring Fair, Frankfurt, W. Germany	Feb. 21–25, 1981	General
6. 5th Forum of Nations, Brussels, Belgium	May 1–13, 1981	General
7. Scandinavian Furniture Fair, Copenhagen, Denmark	May 6–10, 1981	Furniture and accessories
8. Interzum, Cologne, W. Germany	May 22–26, 1981	Construction equipment and furniture
9. Overseas Import Fair, Berlin, W. Germany	Aug. 1981	General
10. Frankfurt International Autumn Fair, Frankfurt, W. Germany	Aug.–Sept. 1981	General
11. Canadian National Exhibition, Toronto, Canada	Aug.–Sept. 1981	General
12. International Leather Week, Offenbach, W. Germany	Aug. 19–Sept. 1, 1981	Leather products
13. International Consumer Goods Fair, Gothenburg, Sweden	Sept. 12–20, 1981	General
14. Spoga '81 (International Trade Fair of Sports goods, camping equipment and garden furniture), Cologne, W. Germany	Sept. 1981	Sports goods, camping equipment and garden furniture

APPENDIX II

References and Further Reading

CHAPTER ONE

Bartels, R. "A Model for Ethics in Marketing." *Journal of Marketing*, January 1967.

Boone, L. E. and Kurtz, D. L. *Foundations of Marketing*. Hinsdale, Illinois: Dryden Press, 1977.

Bowen, H. R. *Social Responsibilities of the Business*. New York: Harper & Row, 1953.

Brandt, W. *et al. North/South—a Programme for Survival: Report of the Independent Commission on International Development Issues*. London: Pan, 1980.

Drucker, P. F. *Managing in Turbulent Times*. London: Pan, 1981.

Foster, D. *Mastering Marketing*. London: Macmillan, 1982.

Kotler, P. *Marketing Management: Analysis, Planning and Control*. Hemel Hempstead: Prentice-Hall, 1980.

Maxwell, R. G. I. *Marketing—A Fresh Approach*. London: Pan, 1983.

CHAPTER TWO

Hout, T., Porter, M. E. and Rudden, E. "How Global Companies Win Out." *Harvard Business Review*, Sept.–Oct. 1982, pp. 98–108.

Keegan, W. J. *Multinational Marketing Management*. Hemel Hempstead: Prentice-Hall, 1980.

Livingstone, J. M. F. *International Marketing Management*. London: Macmillan, 1976.

Porter, M. E. *Competitive Strategy*. New York: Free Press, 1980.

Weinstein, A. K. and Fargher, K. H. F. *Case Studies in International Marketing*. London: Edward Arnold, 1970.

CHAPTER THREE

Boone, L. E. and Kurtz, D. L. *Foundations of Marketing*. Hinsdale, Illinois: Dryden Press, 1977.

Deschampsneufs, H. *Marketing in the Common Market*. London: Pan, 1973.

Dillon, J. *Handbook of International Direct Marketing*. New York: McGraw-Hill, 1976.
Journal of Marketing, Vol. 46, 1982. "Industry Export Performance: Assessment and Prediction."
Quarterly Review of Marketing.
Sommers, M. S. and Kernan, J. B. (eds.) *Comparative Marketing Systems*. New York: Appleton-Century-Crofts, 1968.

CHAPTER FOUR

Bickers, R. T. L. *Marketing in Europe*. Epping: Gower Press, 1971.
Bolt, G. J. *Marketing in the EEC*. London: Kogan Page, 1973.
Channon, D. F. and Jalland, M. *Multinational Strategic Planning*. London: Macmillan, 1979.
Deschampsneufs, H. *Marketing Overseas*. Oxford: Pergamon, 1976.
Posses, F. *Selling to the Americans*. London: Business Books, 1971.
Publications/reports of national and international agencies.

CHAPTER FIVE

Brandt, W. *et al*. *North/South—a Programme for Survival: Report of the Independent Commission on International Development Issues*. London: Pan, 1980.
Export Market Research. International Trade Centre. UNCTAD/GATT.
Reports of World Bank, United Nations and the EEC on various world markets.

CHAPTER SIX

Chisnall, P. M. *Marketing: A Behavioural Analysis*. New York: McGraw-Hill, 1975.
Doyle, P. and Hart, N. A. *Case Studies in International Marketing*. London: Heinemann, 1982.
"International Banking Survey." *The Economist*, March 1984.
Keegan, W. *International Marketing Text and Cases*.
Majaro, S. *International Marketing: A Strategic Approach to World Markets*. London: Allen & Unwin, 1982.
Piercy, N. "Export Marketing Strategy: Can Firms Afford the Key Market Concentration Strategy?" *Quarterly Review of Marketing*, Vol. 9, No. 2, pp. 1–9.
Piercy, N. "Export Marketing Management in Medium-Size British Firms." *International Marketing and Technology Transfer*, March 1984.
Thorelli, H. B. and Becker, H. *International Marketing Strategy*. Oxford: Pergamon, 1980.
Tookey, D. *Export Marketing Decisions*. Harmondsworth: Penguin, 1975.

Turnbull, P. W. and Cunningham, M. I. *International Marketing and Purchasing.* London: Macmillan, 1981.

Wilmshurst, J. *How International Marketing Works.*

CHAPTER SEVEN

Deschampsneufs, H. *Export Made Simple.* London: W. H. Allen, 1977.

Kotler, P. *Marketing Management: Analysis, Planning & Control.* Hemel Hempstead: Prentice-Hall, 1980.

Livingstone, J. M. *International Marketing Management.* London: Macmillan, 1976.

Sewell, J. L. *Marketing and Market Assessment.* London: Routledge & Kegan Paul, 1966.

Wilmshurst, J. *The Fundamentals and Practice of Marketing.* London: Heinemann, 1978.

CHAPTER EIGHT

Ansoff, H. I. *Strategic Management.* London: Macmillan, 1979.

Baker, M. J. *Marketing—An Introductory Text.* London: Macmillan, 1979.

Borden, N. H. "The Concept of the Marketing Mix" in *Science in Marketing.* I. Scwartz (ed.). New York: Wiley, 1965.

Holloway, R. J. and Hancock, R. S. (eds.) *The Environment of Marketing Behaviour—Selection from the Literature.* New York: Wiley, 1964.

Kotler, P. "From Sales Obsession to Marketing Effectiveness." *Harvard Business Review,* Nov.–Dec. 1977, pp. 67–75.

Levitt, T. *Innovation in Marketing.* New York: McGraw-Hill, 1962.

Majaro, S. "The Many Faces of Marketing." *Marketing,* Aug. 1977, pp. 16–18.

Shapiro, B. P. "Improve Distribution with your Promotional Mix," *Harvard Business Review,* Mar.–Apr. 1977, pp. 115–123.

Stapleton, J. (ed.) *Marketing Handbook.* Epping: Gower Press, 1974.

Van Leer, R. K. "Industrial Marketing with a Flair." *Harvard Business Review,* Nov.–Dec. 1976, pp. 117–124.

CHAPTER NINE

Cardozo, R. N. *Product Policy, Cases and Concepts.* Reading, Mass.: Addison-Wesley, 1979.

Davidson, H. "Making an Entrance." *Marketing,* 1st Dec. 1983, pp. 29–30.

Davidson, H. "Building on a Winner." *Marketing,* 24th Nov. 1983, pp. 37–39.

Keegan, W. J. *Multinational Marketing Management.* London: Prentice-Hall, 1974.

Turnbull, P. W. and Cunningham, H. T. (eds.) *International Marketing and Purchasing*. London: Macmillan, 1981.

CHAPTER TEN

Buzzell, R. D. "Can you Standardise Multinational Marketing?" *Harvard Business Review*, Nov.–Dec. 1968, pp. 102–113.

Baker, M. J. *Marketing: an Introductory Text*. London: Macmillan, 1979.

Carson, D. "Comparative Marketing—a New Old Aid." *Harvard Business Review*, May–June 1967, p. 22.

Deschampsneufs, H. *Selling Overseas*. London: Business Publications, 1960.

Drucker, P. F. *Managing in Turbulent Times*. London: Heinemann, 1980.

Duguid, A. and Jaques, E. *Case Studies in Export Organisation*. London: HMSO, 1971.

Holloway, R. J. and Hancock, R. S. *Marketing in a Changing Environment*. New York: Wiley, 1968.

Keegan, W. J. *International Marketing Text and Cases*.

Livingstone, J. M. *International Marketing Management*. London: Macmillan, 1976.

Majaro, S. *International Marketing: Strategic Approach to World Markets*. London: Allen & Unwin, 1982.

Piper, J. R., Jnr. "How US firms evaluate foreign market opportunities." *MSU Business Topics*, Vol. 19 (Summer 1971), p. 14.

Porter, M. E. *Competitive Strategy*. New York: Free Press, 1980.

Thorelli, H. B. (ed.) *International Marketing Strategy*. Harmondsworth: Penguin, 1973.

Tugendhat, C. *The Multinationals*. London: Eyre & Spottiswoode, 1971.

Wilmshurst, J. *The Fundamentals and Practice of Marketing*. London: Heinemann, 1978.

CHAPTER ELEVEN

Cateora, P. R. and Hess, J. M. *International Marketing*. Homewood, Illinois: R. D. Irwin, 1971.

ITC, Geneva, *Export Product Development*.

ITC, Geneva, *Export Market Research*.

CHAPTER TWELVE

Carson, D. *International Marketing—a Comparative Systems Approach*. New York: Wiley, 1967.

Ward, J. J. *The European Approach to United States Markets: Product and Promotion Adaptation by European Multinational Corporations*. New York: Praeger, 1973.

CHAPTER THIRTEEN

British Overseas Trade Board, *Services*.

Cateora, P. R. and Hess, J. M. *International Marketing*. Homewood, Illinois: R. D. Irwin, 1971.

Export Credits Guarantee Department, *Introductory Guide*.

Jefkins, F. *Modern Marketing*. Plymouth: Macdonald & Evans, 1983.

CHAPTER FOURTEEN

Cateora, P. R. and Hess, J. M. *International Marketing*. Homewood, Illinois: R. D. Irwin, 1971.

ECGD booklets and reports.

Leighton, D. S. R. *International Marketing*. New York: McGraw-Hill, 1966.

CHAPTER FIFTEEN

Bickers, R. T. L. *Marketing in Europe*. Epping: Gower Press, 1971.

Channon, D. and Jalland, M. *Multinational Strategic Planning*. London: Macmillan, 1979.

Chisnall, P. M. *Effective Industrial Marketing*. London: Longman, 1977.

Christopher, M., Walters, D. and Williams, G. *Effective Distribution Management*. Bradford: MCB Publications, 1978.

Frain, J. *Transportation and Distribution for European Markets*. London: Butterworths, 1970.

Guirdham, M. *Marketing—The Management of Distribution Channels*. Oxford: Pergamon, 1972.

Kotler, P. *Marketing Management: Analysis, Planning and Control*. London: Prentice-Hall, 1967.

Leighton, D. *International Marketing—Test and Cases*. New York: McGraw-Hill.

Saatchi and Saatchi. *The Observer*, Sunday 29th January 1984.

Stern, L. W. and El-Ansary, A. J. *Marketing Channels*. London: Prentice-Hall, 1977.

Weinstein, A. and Fargher, K. H. F. *Case Studies in International Marketing*. London: Edward Arnold, 1970.

CHAPTER SIXTEEN

Financial Times, changes in exchange rates.

Root, F. R. *Strategic Planning for Export Marketing*. Copenhagen: Einar Harck, 1964.

Tookey, D. *Physical Distribution for Export*. London: Gower Press, 1971.

CHAPTER SEVENTEEN

Cateora, P. R. and Hess, J. M. *International Marketing*. Homewood, Illinois: R. D. Irwin, 1971.
ILO (Geneva), management development reports.
Peters, T. and Waterman, R. H. *In Search of Excellence*. Harper & Row.

CHAPTER EIGHTEEN

Cateora, P. R. and Hess, J. M. *International Marketing*. Homewood, Illinois: R. D. Irwin, 1971.
Hulbert, J. M. and Brandt, W. K. *Formulating Objectives and Evaluating Performance in the Multinational Subsidiary*. Columbia University, American Marketing Association, 1978 Educators Conference Proceedings.
Rodger, L. W. *Marketing in Competitive Economies*. London: Hutchinson, 1965.
Tookey, D. *Export Marketing Decisions*. Harmondsworth: Penguin, 1975.
Weinstein, A. K. and Fargher, K. H. F. *Case Studies in International Marketing*. London: Edward Arnold, 1970.

CHAPTER NINETEEN

CTT (Irish Export Board), annual reports.
BOTB. *Services* (information booklet).
ECGD. *Your Questions Answered*.
Export Europe Branch, BOTB. *Selling to Western Europe*.
SITPRO. Pamphlets covering: *Systematic export documentation*; *Certified invoice overlays*; *Sea way bill*; *Common short form bill of lading*; *Costing guidelines for export administration*; *Computers and international trade documents*.
THE (Technical Help to Exporters). *An Introduction to a Unique Export Advisory Service from BSI*.

CHAPTER TWENTY

Behrman, J. N. *National Interests and the Multinational Enterprise*. London: Prentice-Hall, 1970.
Franko, L. G. *The European Multinationals*. London: Harper & Row, 1976.
Phatak, A. V. *Managing Multinational Corporations*. New York: Praeger, 1974.

Vernon, R. *Sovereignty at Bay.*

CHAPTER TWENTY-ONE

Harmondsworth: Penguin, 1973.
British Overseas Trade Board. *Annual Report 1983.*
Henley Centre for Forecasting. *2002: Britain Plus 25.*
International Monetary Fund. *World Economic Outlook.*
Tessler, A. "Alternative Strategies and the Key Market Principle" in *Successful Export Strategy.* Proceedings of a conference sponsored by the London Chamber of Commerce and Industry and the Institute of Export. London: Graham & Trotman, 1977.
United Nations Publication. *World Economic Survey.*

Case Studies

The object of outlining some short business histories in international marketing is to give the student some feel for the export story, rather than the chapter-by-chapter approach. It should also be stressed that these are true-life business histories, but they are a poor substitute for meeting the very innovative business leaders themselves. These are the real national heroes, the wealth creators, and the hope of the unemployed, from whatever country they emerge.

In this appendix, three cases from developing countries and three from the British Isles are outlined briefly to inspire the existing and potential international marketer, as well as the student of international marketing.

1. A CRAFT, GIFTWARE AND SILK-EXPORTING FIRM IN THAILAND

NOTE: This brief business history is typical of many innovative Third World initiatives. It shows the key role for a middleman in a country with many small producers where quality control is necessary and exporting skills are scarce. (*See also* Appendix I.)

A Thai craft and giftware firm was established by a girl in her mid-twenties, who had an eye for quality in terms of Thailand's craft and woodwork products. She also had a keen eye for export opportunities through regular contact with the Export Service Centre in Bangkok.

The start-up was simple. With two lorries, and using a shed at the end of her garden as a warehouse, she helped the first drivers in the achieving of good quality control standards. With the help of a younger brother and two sisters, she managed to fill her first overseas orders, while keeping her stocks to a minimum because of the modest size of her warehouse. With the help of the Export Service Centre, she began to make personal contact with customers in North America and Europe at a rate of two visits per year; during each trip she covered both markets. She maintained a strict cash flow and demanded prompt payment, based on a minimum order of 100 items and $2,000 cash order minimum. This, she felt, made exporting worth while.

After five years, she had ten lorries, collecting a range of products from producers all over Thailand. The driver in each case also carefully vetted the quality on collection. The range included silk products, wooden products and other giftware, at keen prices. She was able to purchase another 1½ acres adjacent to her original shed, and now has additional warehouse space. This young lady has shown the best of business acumen and creativity in selecting her product range, consolidating her export market contacts and image, and planning a phased growth, mainly financing the developments from her business success.

2. A BATIK BUSINESS IN SRI LANKA

NOTE: This Sri Lanka export case history gives insight into a start-up project by an art and design graduate, keeping his expenses to a minimum at the initial stage, and proving he could produce a quality product. The project also shows the importance of consolidating initial export contacts and visiting the market, irrespective of distance.

A young art graduate, at the age of twenty-four, set up a small batik business in a shed in Colombo, Sri Lanka, in the early 1970s. At first, he had just his own design ideas, and three girls working on the batiks.

After one or two local displays in tourist hotels, and help from the Sri Lanka Export Promotion Agency, he was able to achieve two or three export orders in the United States. Gradually, these initial orders were repeated, and the export network of contacts grew to the point where he had some twenty girls working in an extended shed.

Two developments then took place. He made two visits to the United States, Canadian and European markets, which meant that he now had orders from American, Canadian, West German and Scandinavian customers. This led to the second development—the movement to a new factory out in the country north of Colombo, which meant, after some six years, employment for 300 girls, a marketing manager and an accountant. By the end of the 1970s, some of the most beautiful batiks leaving Sri Lanka were his own personally designed products, and over 75 per cent of his production was for export markets, mainly North America and Europe.

He believed in visiting his markets personally twice a year, and had decided to consolidate his four export markets before extending them further to the United Kingdom and France. The hallmarks of his success might be summarised as follows:

(a) his own constant creativity and innovation;
(b) his closeness to his customers, visiting and listening to them many thousand of miles from home; and
(c) his dedicated work-force whom he knew on first-name terms, and who worked in small groups with dedication and flexibility.

3. THE TINKABI TRACTOR COMPANY, SWAZILAND

NOTE: This Swaziland project gives some insight into the need to adapt products to particular environments, particularly Third World environments. This adaptation is then followed by a comprehensive product testing plan before the exporting phase.

In 1973, two brothers from the United Kingdom were asked by the industrial development organisation in Swaziland to come out and develop a Third World tractor in the Ezelweni valley. From initial research it became apparent that 60 per cent of faults in farm machinery, particularly tractors, were electrical. This led to the first fundamental decision that this special tractor for developing countries would have *no electrics*—a mechanical machine only. This meant avoiding 60 per cent of the faults, as an electric tractor would have proved impossible, given the absence of electrical garage repair networks in developing countries.

Other ergonomic features included:

(*a*) a high ground clearance—at least 3 ft (approx. 1m) to allow for rocky terrain;

(*b*) wide wheelbase to give stability for uneven and sloping hillside work;

(*c*) seven component accessories for flexibility in all-round farm tasks, including a small guider or crushing machine;

(*d*) a robust engine imported from India, and strong mechanical parts which could mean repair by local handymen or the farmer.

All of this was priced at a modest £1,800. Before exporting, a product testing plan was organised which involved 300 Swazi farmers testing 300 tractors, giving weekly reports on performance. After one year of tests the reports from the 300 farmers were very encouraging. It took all of the five-year contract to develop and test the tractors.

In 1979, some twenty tractors were exported to the Kenyan market, and hopes were high for further export orders. However, while the project was strong on development, production and testing, further strength was needed in the marketing and exporting side. Anxiety was felt for credit control and repayment possibilities from some African countries. It was felt that selected developing countries in Africa should be the first export market targets. Asian and Latin American countries could be later targets.

4. CU PRODUCTS (NORTHERN IRELAND) LTD.

Introduction
This company has been attempting to export copper giftware (hand-made) to the United States and German markets. The approaches to the two export markets have been quite distinct. An interesting feature about the approach to the American market is the development of a joint export marketing plan with two other companies, involving the establishment of a marketing and distribution centre in the Boston area, for initial penetration of the New England markets, aiming at the Irish ethnic groups.

The owner

The owner, Mr Jim Dowds, is a Northern Ireland man, who learned the copperware craft in South Africa. He returned to Northern Ireland in the 1970s, and his company now employs thirty-three people, with annual sales of £500,000. In 1981 and 1982, he streamlined his production process, while maintaining a hand-made finish. This increased throughput enabled him to consider potential export markets.

The markets

In terms of the United States, after some initial visits, he is liaising with two other companies producing a range of compatible products, with a view to establishing a marketing and distribution centre in the United States. One of the limiting factors of going through the normal range of middlemen was the increased marginal impact on retail price, leading to an inability to compete with products from South East Asia.

The concept of a marketing and distribution centre is aimed at a more direct approach to the final consumer, thereby leading to a more competitive price. Costs of a marketing and distribution centre in the Boston area will initially include a marketing manager and secretary. The possibility of locating in a free trade zone is also being considered. Contacts made as a result of an earlier exhibition in Boston were responsible for an initial order of $50,000.

In the case of the British mainland and West German markets, a more traditional approach to exporting has been developed. This small company has the usual problem of organising its priorities and management team between the three markets outlined above. Consolidation of the United Kingdom market would appear to be the first priority under the new sales manager, while the United States and German markets are being further investigated.

5. PLANNING THE DEVELOPMENT OF A SMALL BUSINESS: DATAC CONTROL LIMITED

(Author: Cyril Kerr, Chief Executive, Datac Control Ltd., Dublin.)

In June 1981, there were three people in their late twenties sitting in an empty 4,000 square foot IDA (Industrial Development Authority) factory unit in Pearse Street, Dublin. All they had was an idea, a company called DATAC Control Ltd., lots of enthusiasm and an empty order book. Who would have believed then that, within two-and-a-half years, we would have beaten the Japanese in Hong Kong, be exporting sophisticated computer-based systems to Africa, have a profitable and on-going export business to West Germany, and be absolute market leaders in our chosen area of activity—Ireland. The answer: probably no one—except ourselves.

With the advent of microelectronics, the small enterprise can now operate in areas which were traditionally the preserve of multinationals or giant corporations. An emerging innovative electronics company can identify and capture for itself a market niche, where its flexibility and ingenuity in its approach to problem-solving represent the key tools to its success in increasing its market share.

I would like now to describe some of the successes and headaches encountered in implementing the planning and development of a small business enterprise such as DATAC.

Plans

The start-up plan involved three distinct phases in the first twelve months:

(a) sourcing the product;
(b) bringing the product to market;
(c) establishing credibility.

The strategy of turning this idea into a viable enterprise was formulated in late 1980. The first decision to be taken was whether DATAC should operate just on an agency basis, earning a commission, or perhaps as a software buying house, buying in the hardware and just writing the software.

However, I believed that DATAC could offer a better service and a full product with all aspects of quality and delivery under our control, if we were to set up a manufacturing facility.

Sourcing the product

In order to leap-frog from the idea stage to the actual manufacture of the product, it was decided not to invest in a long research and development programme, but to license a well-proven product. I located a West German company which had a customer base identical to that which DATAC regarded as the most suitable in the short term.

The next step was to prepare a business plan, expressed in terms of financial budgets for the first three years. This outline business plan was then presented to the IDA's Enterprise Development Unit in November 1980. After a short series of meetings, we received outline approval from them. Because they were apparently convinced of the viability of the project, they were determined to optimise the start-up conditions. The IDA then effectively crucified my plan. After this gruelling experience, a comprehensive financing, project management and development plan was agreed. With IDA approval agreed, the task of financing the project began.

With our perceived credibility problem at the pre-start-up stage, I felt there was no point in approaching any potential sources of venture capital, and so I raised the seed capital from family and friends. Having raised the necessary seed capital for start-up, we were now faced with realising our ideas. Unless you can implement plans, and make them happen, they have no value whatsoever.

I regarded the ability to deliver the product within a short period as crucial. The skills and technical know-how were not available to us in Ireland. This precluded an R & D programme, since it would involve a substantial investment in manpower and resources, delay the launch of the product and eat into the start-up capital. To overcome these problems, I negotiated a licensing deal with the German company. The most significant advantage of this deal to an emerging indigenous electronics company in Ireland is that, by launching a well-proven product, some of the credibility problems are immediately overcome.

Credibility did not only concern convincing the market of our technical know-how and ability to deliver, but was also of importance to our relationship with the IDA, shareholders, the banks and even suppliers, although negotiating terms with suppliers in the height of a recession was not difficult. To attract good quality employees, DATAC had to appear to be a viable enterprise. Since our business involved the supply of capital equipment which customers expected to use for at least fifteen years, it was essential to convince them that DATAC was here to stay and would provide a back-up service in years to come.

Other than the purchase of software development systems, the second single biggest item of expenditure in the pre-production days involved the modification of the IDA building unit to provide a reception area, conference room and a number of offices. From a marketing point of view, I felt it was absolutely essential to provide the office area as part of our efforts to establish credibility and to create a mature image overnight. Can you imagine trying to sell £100,000 worth of equipment sitting at a desk planted in the middle of an empty factory unit?

Despite the many advantages the licensing deal brought, the up-front cash payments ate into the start-up capital. Licensing deals are not eligible for grant aid. To stem the flow of cash to the Germans, I negotiated a deal whereby we would manufacture the product for them. Within three months of production start-up, we were shipping our first sample exports to Germany. The immediate benefit of this strategy was that we generated a positive inward flow of deutschmarks which more than covered the licence fees. Furthermore, the export orders provided continuous employment for the production staff.

Our customer in Germany had an intimate knowledge of the product, and we got an immediate feedback on quality. This helped tremendously to overcome start-up problems.

The speed with which we actually moved from the licence negotiations into production convinced the IDA and banks of our ability to perform.

Because of the high number of units we were producing, we now had large-scale buying power, and our suppliers sat up and took notice. We could afford to be selective in our choice of suppliers, and were able to negotiate substantial quantity discounts on some components.

Bringing the product to the market

Having shown that we could get the show on the road, the job of selling the product was tackled next. DATAC is a very marketing-oriented company.

Our marketing strategy in early days was split into three stages:

(a) ability to perform;
(b) educate the market;
(c) gain market share.

To convince potential users of our ability to perform, we adopted the policy of keeping a high profile in the technical press. We also exhibited at our first Electronics Show in the Royal Dublin Society within five months of start-up. All equipment on display had been manufactured by us, and was ready for installation in the customers' plants.

The areas of application for DATAC's products were still relatively unknown in Ireland. To overcome this, we organised training seminars and system demonstrations for consultant engineers, government department officials, local authority engineers and other potential customers. The strategy we had was to educate the market and then to hold on to it. We wanted to achieve a solid DATAC/user relationship and make our customers believe in the technology.

At this stage, we regarded gaining market share as more crucial than profits. We targeted the market very closely, and began an aggressive marketing campaign to win our first orders.

Perhaps at this stage we should say a word about the actual product. Let us first look at the stages of manufacture.

DATAC designs and manufactures high quality monitoring and control systems for use by electricity boards, water boards, gas boards, oil companies, railways and telecommunication authorities.

The first stage of manufacture involves the loading of components on to PCBs (printed circuit boards). They are then soldered into place. After this the PCBs are sent for test, where we use automatic test equipment to ensure a 100 per cent quality control check. In the mechanical and electrical assembly area, cabinets and control panels are assembled and wired up. The finished systems are then programmed by the software development engineers, and a complete system test is then carried out before delivery to site.

The CIE (Irish Transport Authority) Bray-to-Howth Suburban Electrification Scheme was the first project we got involved in. DATAC supplied the back-up remote control and monitoring system to provide such functions as raising and lowering the level crossings, etc. This was followed by a number of contracts with the Department of Energy and the Electricity Supply Board.

In the second year of operation, market penetration in Ireland was the prime objective. We still regarded increasing the market share as the most crucial aspect of our business development plan. The experience gained in the first twelve months really paid off when in June 1982 we were awarded the prestigious contract to supply the complete computer-based monitoring and control system for the Bord Gais Cork-to-Dublin Gas Pipeline Project. This contract represented a major milestone in the development of our business. It was won in the face of stiff international competition. Not only was it the largest single order we had handled, but the prestige attached to this project put DATAC into the international league of computer-based monitoring and control system manufacturers. Subsequently, we won a large contract for a similar system from Dublin Gas.

In order to win work in areas where DATAC was relatively unknown, we adopted the strategy of "piggybacking" on to large contracts by operating as subcontractors for work with the county councils. In Co Kerry, the North East Kerry Water Supply Scheme is a prestigious project in which DATAC supplies monitoring systems located at a number of reservoirs, water towers and pumping stations. The operation of the Listowel water treatment plant is automatically controlled by our equipment. The operational information on the water supply is reported back to the county council offices in Tralee.

Towards the end of our second year of business, DATAC had not only established credibility, but had achieved a high market share. The next phase of development was to expand into export markets.

At this stage, we knew that as a small business, with a limited marketing budget, we could not afford to shoot off in all directions. Again, we targeted the markets very closely. As a first step, we took part in meetings and exhibitions in the United Kingdom. In my opinion, to attack the United Kingdom market for sales on that market—which would be mostly to government authorities—DATAC would need a strong United Kingdom presence. As this was not then possible, we specifically decided to view the United Kingdom market as a "through market", by which I mean we wished to "piggyback" on to United Kingdom contractors and consultants for overseas work. We received a number of enquiries in this way, and through the Crown Agents based in Whitehall, we were invited to tender for two sizeable projects in Hong Kong.

By coincidence, the Irish Export Board invited us at the same time to participate in an electronics and instrumentation exhibition in Shanghai in the People's Republic of China. I had the opportunity on that trip to spend two days in negotiations with the Water Supplies Department of Hong Kong, and we were subsequently awarded both contracts. The piggyback technique had paid off.

To the small business enterprise, the technique of piggybacking on to large overseas contracts, using multinationals as front men, is immediately attractive. The multinational company offers marketing strengths and instant access to faraway markets. On the financing side, DATAC can agree its own payment terms with the main contractor, who on the other hand can offer project financing to the customer. DATAC saves the cost of performance bonds and special insurance policies. The difficulties of arranging letters of credit and currency exchange risks are avoided.

From the marketing point of view, many projects are awarded on a turn-key basis, which may involve civil works or mechanical and electrical plant which are outside the scope of normal DATAC business activities. Many large multinationals will have the internal organisational structures to handle such projects, but may lack the necessary expertise in the specialist electronics control system area, which DATAC can provide. Through the established network of contacts, which such contractors have, DATAC receives market exposure which would otherwise take years and years to build up.

Our approach to each contracting company is individualised, that is, we tailor our relationship on a job-by-job basis. In this way, restrictive commitments, which could exclude doing business with other companies, is avoided.

In addition to the Hong Kong contracts, we are now tendering for other projects in South East Asia worth around US$2 million. We have visited this market three times in the last year, and will continue to concentrate our marketing efforts there. We are presently manufacturing a large number of systems for the Zambian Telecommunications Corporation in Lusaka. In this project, our systems are used to monitor and control the backbone radio network of the Zambian PTT. This order was also won through an international corporation.

We believe our strategy in the export market has worked overall. Our sales in this our third year have grown by 50 per cent, and exports will account for approximately 45 per cent of turnover. It is interesting to note that the contracts awarded to us in the first two years were all listed in the original business development plan submitted to the IDA. This helped to establish further our credibility with the banks and the IDA.

Finance

Let us look now at the financial side of things. I soon learned that financing a project may be one of the most difficult tasks of doing business. In the first year of operation, the seed capital was mostly sufficient to fund the day-to-day activities with relatively little need for borrowing—stage payments on contracts combined with regular exports to Germany offset licensing costs and eased the burden.

The second year of the company's life was marked by rapid growth, which brought with it all the usual growing pains, in particular cash flow problems. Additional capital was required to meet the demand for our products. With an established customer base and a healthy set of accounts, we were in a strong bargaining position with the banks. Nevertheless, without the IDA loan guarantee scheme, further borrowing would probably not have been possible.

Irregularity of payments from customers, combined with the large number of contracts on hand and the addition of new staff and developing expertise caused cash flow headaches. The strategy of compounding this growth, by increasing market share, and expanding into new markets, by investing heavily in marketing for future projects, together with the on-going development programme for new software, all had an effect on the bottom line performance in the second year. However, the foundation for further growth was established, and within the first three months of the third year, orders on hand represented 60 per cent of forecasted sales for the year.

As payment terms on exports were bad from a cash-flow point of view, we decided to avail of the Industrial Credit Corporation's Working Capital for Export Scheme. Business plans were revised for the coming twelve months, and presented to the banks, and re-financing was arranged. It was also decided to introduce internal management strategies to ease cash flow headaches. Trade credit arrangements were renegotiated with our suppliers. Stock control was improved by introducing computerisation of stores and purchasing, and we are attempting to accelerate the collection of accounts receivable, with some success.

At the initial stage, we had a lack of internal expertise, and DATAC availed of the services of Stokes, Kennedy and Crowley Ltd., to establish accounting and reporting systems, prepare financial reports, budgets and forecasts, and provide general financial advice. The Irish Productivity Centre was hired to prepare regular management accounts. With the Management Information System, it was now possible for us to control the business to anticipate cash flow peaks and troughs, and to monitor performance on a project-by-project basis.

DATAC is now reaching a stage of maturity with a comprehensive organisational structure in place, well-known prestigious contracts under the belt, and an aggressive marketing campaign yielding dividends. We must now look at our future plans.

At present we are considering what form of expansion should be chosen—whether to set up divisions which are inexpensive to start and relatively easy to close, or subsidiaries which can provide new business ventures with identities of their own, while still remaining under our direct control, or finally whether to set up new companies, which are totally separate from the existing structure, the advantage here being we could de-emphasise ties to the existing product and customer base.

Our future plans, particularly in the export market, may involve joint ventures in different countries. We may have to set up a subsidiary in South East Asia, if the business there develops to the extent we anticipate.

Review

We are now approaching the end of our third year of operations. When I look back on the development of our company, I can see that many of our original plans did actually come to fruition. However, I never anticipated the range of difficulties we have had to overcome in this period. The business plan has been revised more than once, and will continue to be revised in the future.

Without a doubt, the commitment and dedication of a number of key employees has been one of the main contributing factors to our success. In this context, I find it rather disappointing that the recent Finance Bill did nothing to help the rewarding of key personnel. The restrictions on the qualifying individual for the purposes of the Business Expansion Scheme are too limiting for a high-tech company such as ours; the high level of personal taxation makes it difficult for us to keep good young engineers in Ireland. We must be able to reward enterprise.

In summary, planning and implementing the development of DATAC Control Ltd. has been a strenuous but satisfying experience. We have established ourselves on the Irish market, and are making good inroads into the export markets. We hope that growth in turnover will be accompanied by a growth in profits. The emergence of a native Irish-owned electronics company such as DATAC is something which we believe to be important in its own small way for the future of the Irish economy, and we feel proud that a small group of young Irish people, based in the heart of Dublin, can tackle and beat many multinational giants in the home and export markets.

6. STRATEGIC PLANNING AMID UNCERTAINTY: VERBATIM LTD.

(Author: Nicky Hertery, Chief Executive, Verbatim Ltd.)

My intention in presenting this case study is to show how strategic decisions taken in the past have resulted in Verbatim becoming today the number one manufacturer of flexible magnetic media and to show how our choice of goals and actions have contributed to this fact.

As you know, the successful outcome of any strategic planning exercise depends on an understanding of every aspect of the existing situation in a business, and developing creative options for dealing with each aspect. Providing these options implies a choice on the part of those people who are influential in choosing from the options, which, therefore, can result in significantly variable performances for a company and its various units. By having a formal strategic planning process, a corporation can reduce the degree of variation in performances, and help to optimise choices to the mutual benefit of the corporation and the decision-makers.

Verbatim has worked consistently on a process of critically reviewing its position within its markets, its technologies and its competition, with the intention of assessing its opportunities, threats, strengths and weaknesses. We believe this has paid off in terms of performance and in this case study I will show you in outline the various strategies we have applied as a corporation, emphasising how and where we in Limerick have been influenced by these processes, and how we in turn have influenced the development of the corporation and Limerick. I will also show, in summary, how our financial performance has developed over the period in question.

Not everything we have done resulted from careful planning. Some actions were the result of circumstances as we found ourselves in them, but doubtlessly we would not have achieved the degree of success we have, had we not planned the major part of our business.

Verbatim is today *the* world's leading manufacturer of flexible magnetic media, supplying what are more commonly called "floppy discs" to ever-growing and changing markets through multiple distribution channels world-wide. We have become *the* media company, through having specific strategies such as:

(*a*) strong financial objectives which are constantly reviewed to strengthen the corporation;

(*b*) commitment to technology leadership;

(*c*) early introduction of new products to meet market demands;

(*d*) continuing productivity improvements from automation and cost-improvement programmes;

(*e*) commitment to quality and service;

(*f*) prudent diversification plans into businesses complementary to flexible media;

(*g*) a dedication to achievement.

These strategic objectives give rise to a hierarchy of tasks and priorities, all of which are interdependent and oriented towards satisfying both existing and future customers' needs.

Our product range includes 5¼ in. mini-diskettes; 8 in. diskettes; ½ in. tape cartridges and maxi and mini cassettes for digital information recording in all types of computers and electronic instruments. We also provide software duplicating services worldwide, and are about to launch a 3½ in. micro disc to serve this newest and fast-growing sector of the market.

Our present facilities include seven manufacturing plants around the world, located in Sunnyvale, California; Limerick, Ireland; Charlotte, North Carolina; Tokyo, Japan; Melbourne, Australia; Nogales, Mexico; and Manaus, Brazil. Only Sunnyvale and Limerick have media-coating capabilities, which between them will serve all our needs for magnetic media. These manufacturing plants and sales offices are located close to our major markets throughout the world to serve a sales volume of £180 million, with an employment of just under 3,000 people.

Our first manufacturing plant was established in Sunnyvale, California, in 1969, and grew to become a nine-building, 400,000 sq. ft. manufacturing complex over the next eight years. By 1976 it became obvious that continuing success required entering markets outside North America, and after considering the implications of this course, it was decided to set up manufacturing plants in Ireland, Australia and Japan initially.

Our first off-shore venture then was established in Limerick in November 1978 in temporary premises, while a 60,000 sq. ft. purpose-built plant was being constructed. This was a disc-finishing plant to which discs and unassembled jackets were sent for burnishing, certification, formatting, packout and distribution.

As events followed in rapid succession, we went to Melbourne, Australia, which was set up in November 1980, and which today finishes 8 in. diskettes and 5¼ in. mini-discs for Australia and New Zealand.

Our next step was the setting up of a Japanese operation in 1980, which for strategic reasons subsequently became a joint venture with Mitsubishi in 1983.

All of these developments required an improved organisational structure and approach to management, and we finalised the establishment of a corporate organisation in Sunnyvale in October 1982 to provide a centralised focus for all our international activities.

As the markets in Europe grew, we in Limerick foresaw the need for extra media-coating capacity. In preparation for an operations review, we looked at how this might be done. A study carried out by the Limerick management showed the economic sense of setting up a coating line in Limerick and their recommendation was accepted by the parent plant.

This is a particularly important fact from a "strategy" point of view which cemented Ireland's future for some time to come, and on which I would like to dwell for a few moments.

Magnetic media manufacturing is essentially a four-technology process involving magnetics, wet chemistry, electronics and mechanics. The magnetics and wet chemistry parts are very much a "black magic" business, involving as they do years of experimentation and experience in developing formulae for the magnetic oxides. This is a highly specialised part of the business and there are not many magnetic media-coating plants in the world, let alone in any one company (approximately eight world-wide). Having this capability in Ireland to meet European, Middle East and African markets means that future expansion of European manufacturing should only involve down-stream activities, much as Verbatim in Limerick was initially.

So from a strategy point of view, to ensure longevity and influence over your future, go to the front end of your technology for future investment in Ireland. This type of investment also begets R & D to support it, and to digress momentarily, it is my belief that Ireland's future lies not solely in R & D operations *per se*, but in having technologies which require R & D for their future.

Thus, in November 1981, work commenced on our media-coating plant, and was completed in January 1983. This second facility includes a research and development centre, where process and equipment development work is carried out and I will talk about this work later.

This coating line is the only other coating line in the company, and represents a high confidence in Ireland. As you can imagine, we are particularly proud of this facility which now meets all our immediate European requirements, and also serves the Japanese and Australian media requirements, and those of our Irish subsidiary in Manaus, Brazil.

In April 1983 we opened the first of four 100,000 sq. ft. manufacturing facilities in Charlotte, North Carolina, which will generate cost efficiencies in bringing Verbatim's products to the market-place. At around the same time, we moved our cassette production equipment into a new modern facility in Nogales, Mexico. This move has freed up production space for extra 5¼ in. mini-disc production in Sunnyvale.

A joint venture with Mac Industrial Ltda, called Verbatim Dos Amazonas Ltda, started in Manaus, Brazil, in late 1983 to serve the South American market, which we estimate as being the sixth largest in the world for our products.

As the market for software duplication got started and continued to grow, we introduced "data encore", a software duplicating facility in Sunnyvale in October 1983 to serve the United States market. We in Limerick had a "skunk house" operation going in the meantime, and have since set this up on a formal basis with its own 10,000 sq. ft. of work space to meet the Irish, United Kingdom and European software duplication markets. Already we have received significant orders from overseas export markets and software houses throughout Europe, and plan to employ seventeen people over the next six to nine months. This will be a capital-intensive operation, with a high level of investment in equipment.

Based on decisions taken in 1982, we are presently building our third manufacturing plant in Limerick. This will be completed on 1st January 1985, and will house an expanded 5¼ in. mini-disc capacity and our automated 3½ in. micro-disc manufacturing line. These developments will maintain our position as the leading media producer in Europe, offering a full range of magnetic disc products.

Having a target of achieving a sales revenue of $1 billion by the end of the decade means we have to continue to provide manufacturing capacity to meet our requirements. This will be done at the three major manufacturing sites in Sunnyvale, Limerick and Charlotte, along with extra finishing plants close-in to the market, which for Limerick means going on to the European mainland.

As Limerick is now the European manufacturing headquarters, we have the task of exploring what is required, and in fact work has already commenced on this question. We see the need for plants located near to our markets to ensure speed in service and delivery.

To help us deal with the uncertainties of market size, the rate of growth, the introduction of alternative products, product improvements, technology improvements or competitor action in any of these areas, the company has set down specific operating principles to keep itself focused on its purposes. These global principles are communicated throughout the company, as is our corporate mission statement.

Continuous growth demands a controlled management approach. For Verbatim, this means having a centralised treasury function, a decentralised management information system, decentralised manufacturing responsibility, a formal planning process, a strong internal auditing function, and the judicious use of management consultants to provide independent opinions. Our investment in growth is done through a controlled management process which ensures we meet our customers' needs, and thereby maximise our opportunities and returns.

We are constantly seeking new effective marketing and distribution channels. Brand promotion is a particularly important activity, and a considerable amount of our resources goes into advertising our brand names, such as Datalife, Optima and Verex.

The growth demands human resource development, especially managers. To satisfy this demand, we have extensive key manager development programmes, college recruiting, and management incentive plans. A formal succession planning programme helps to identify candidates for development and ensures we have the right people in the right place at the right time.

Research and development is a cost which has to be managed to ensure return on resources. Capital expansion programmes are supported where possible solely out of profits.

A market that is growing at 47 per cent cumulative growth rate (some would say 65 per cent), as the 5¼ in. market is, will never be left alone for long, and new competitors are entering almost monthly. When we started in Ireland in 1978, there were only four serious contenders for a market which was a fraction of today's size. Now there are some thirty-four suppliers. Two additions in 1984 so far include Polaroid and Kodak.

Our market share throughout 1982 and 1983 remained at a healthy 37 per cent, and we intend to improve on this over the coming times. Many of the latter-day entrants do not have the technical support for their products that an organisation such as Verbatim can provide, and in time they will be faced with extinction for want of a market leader position.

The continuing growth in demand for floppy discs is fuelled by what we term the "micro-computer software approach", which generates a spin-off demand for discs as software writers come up with new spread-sheet programs like Visicalc, Multiplan and Lotus 1–2–3; data-base systems like DB-Management; word-processing packages and similar program packages.

Looking specifically at the way in which the market for 5¼ in. mini-discs is structured and changing, we can see that as the large and small business sectors reduce in size but grow in volume, the education and home computer sectors are increasing, as is the government sector. It is interesting to note that the United States government and large account-ancy firms such as Peat, Marwick and Mitchell are putting together planned introductions of micro or personal computers for their executives. The early success of the Apple Macintosh is attributable in part to Peat, Marwick and Mitchell's decision to buy 3,500 Macintoshes for use in their 200 offices around the United States.

All of this means that by 1988, Verbatim will have a $1 billion sales potential which we intend to achieve. This revenue will be generated from existing products and products yet to be brought to market, but on which a lot of R & D is being carried out.

Strategic management involves monitoring and understanding trends, and so we constantly review the sales performance of our product lines on, for example, an individual basis, and by sales channels, as we fully analyse what is happening.

Again, from a strategy point of view, we have been influential in establishing the industrial standard for the micro-disc by having our own specific strategy of interrelating with the drive manufacturers. This en-sured that the ANSI or industry standard was met through our active participation in the Industry Committee, which has plumped for a 3½ in. disc with 500 KB storage capacity. As already mentioned, our third plant in Limerick will be ready for this development.

Any strategy for a technologically based business can only bear fruit when it is supported by an active research and development programme. Research and development for Verbatim is an essential activity, when one considers the technologies of high-density flexible discs, which demand expertise and continuous research into magnetic properties, chemistry, manufacturing process and substrate film. Our R & D strategy ensures that we will be totally to the front in all areas of new technology and product development, as we concentrate on issues such as durability of media, packing greater amounts of information on smaller discs, reducing costs and finding new applications for our products. Our level of investment in research and development has been growing through the years from 3 per cent of sales to 9 per cent in this fiscal year. This puts us in the highest category of research and development expenditure within the industry.

The amount of research and development spending in Ireland for February 1984 is almost half a million pounds. When we started in Limerick in 1979, there was no plan for research and development in Ireland. As we experienced various production problems, process development became a necessity, and funds were made available locally to support this. In 1983, we received IDA support for an enhanced stand-alone research and development effort. This is housed in a purpose-built 9,500 sq. ft. technical centre, and takes its place within the company's overall research and development programmes. Individual projects have been allocated to the various R & D sites, and in Limerick we are now specifically responsible for certain aspects of media development and diagnostic products. Our efforts in Limerick to date have resulted in a diagnostic disc and an alignment disc for which world-wide patents were taken out. We have also developed a micro-processor-controlled image digitiser for an automated product dimension measurement system to ensure product quality specifications are exceeded.

Our immediate corporate strategy within R & D today is centred about ensuring we can accommodate higher recording densities, smaller diskette size, software duplication services and ½ in. tape cartridges.

In many ways, therefore, Verbatim has its business objectives and strategies crisply defined, so as to ensure its growth in the magnetic media market, to supply quality products at competitive prices to end users, original equipment manufacturers and distributors world-wide and achieve the return of an industry leader.

Obviously success does not just happen. It has to be planned for and planning by definition is a strategic activity. However, the proof of this pudding is in the financial results. We have had a 400 per cent increase in net sales over 1979 to 1983. Our gross margin has improved by 30 per cent over this period with a continuous decline in annual untaxed profit. Net income also grew over the same five-year period. Our cash flow has varied over this five-year period, as our fixed asset addition costs were absorbed. The return on total capital has generally met the target of 20 per cent and is well on target for this year. Debt as a percentage of total capital has reduced to below the 30 per cent corporate limit; all of which have resulted in an average return on equity of 21 per cent over the five-year period 1978–1983.

So, in summary, Verbatim has strategically placed itself to become successful in the rapidly growing market for flexible magnetic media through its formal review and planning process. This has resulted in specific strategies in Limerick:

(a) getting into media coating;
(b) introducing research and development;
(c) having an active vendor education programme to achieve and exceed quality standards;
(d) investing in facilities and people ahead of time;
(e) meeting market demand through extending our product range by bringing in micro-disc and software duplication services;
(f) ensuring all of these efforts are measured against specific financial objectives.

Doing this has given us our commanding position in this market and through this we remain fully committed to enhancing shareholder value, maintaining the leading position, developing new products and facilities in time to lever our 5¼ in. product position and the emerging 3½ in. market through innovative marketing programmes.

Verbatim has a potential $1 billion sales by the end of the decade of which 25 per cent will be achieved by Verbatim (Ireland). This $250 million entity will be twice the corporate size at the end of the fiscal year 1983. Limerick's management is challenged with this growth potential, and it is only through strategic planning that this can be controlled and achieved and with strategic planning we will do it.

Index